ESSAY PRESS

SINGING IN MAGNETIC HOOFBEAT

ESSAYS, PROSE TEXTS,

INTERVIEWS AND A LECTURE

1991–2007

EDITED AND WITH AN INTRODUCTION

BY TAYLOR BRADY

AFTERWORD BY ANDREW JORON

ESSAY

WILL ALEXANDER

SINGING IN MAGNETIC HOOFBEAT

PRESS

Published by Essay Press 208 Utica Street Ithaca, New York 14850
www.essaypress.org Design and composition by Quemadura
Printed on acid-free, recycled paper in the United States of America
ISBN 978-0-9791189-7-5 FIRST EDITION

5 4 3 2 1

Some of these texts have previously appeared in the following journals,
anthologies, and books: *Apex of the M*, *Beyond Baroque Magazine*,
Callaloo, *Conjunctions*, *Electric Church* by K. Curtis Lyle, *The Jivin'
Ladybug*, *Lipstick Eleven*, *Milk Magazine*, *Mr. Knife, Miss Fork*, *O•blek:
Writing from the New Coast*, *The Poetry Project Newsletter*, *Ribot*,
River City, *Third Mind: Creative Writing Through Visual Art*,
Tripwire, *Ur-Vox*, and *Witz*. The author, editor and publishers wish
to thank the editors of these publications for their support.

Publication of this book was made possible in part through support
from the New York State Council on the Arts with the support of
Governor Andrew Cuomo and the New York State Legislature

State of the Arts

NYSCA

TO THE AFRICAN DIASPORA ALIVE

WITH THE SELF OF RE-DISCOVERY

THE WING OF IMAGINAL AFRICAN ANTI-GRAVITY

A RELENTLESS METEORITICS

. . . from 5 million years ago to the glacial thaw 10,000 years ago, Africa almost unilaterally peopled and influenced the rest of the world.

CHEIKH ANTA DIOP

EDITOR'S NOTE

Singing in Magnetic Hoofbeat collects nearly seventeen years of essays and other prose writings by Will Alexander. As a document of the evolving scope and acuity of Alexander's thought and practice of his own poetic writing, engagements with surrealism and the literatures of the African diaspora, addresses to public and community occasion, readings of his poetic peers and influences, and immersion in an effort to think African-American literary and artistic practice "outside the Western box," I hope that it will prove as indispensable to scholars and general readers as it has proven generative to my own imagining of a poetics.

In a note attached to the initial packet of typescript and photocopied text with which this project started, Alexander compares his "discovery" and subsequent practice of the essay, beginning in the early 90s, to the instant documentation of present reality possible in snapshot photography. It would be a mistake, though, to read this characterization of the work as license to treat these texts as casual, dispensable adjuncts to the stunning and unique body of poetry that Alexander has produced during the same period. The necessity of documenting the exact constellation of intellectual, cultural and political forces informing the development of the poetry at a given moment imposes a discipline on this work that requires writer and reader to uncover more and different potentialities within the practices of the essay. One might be tempted to read Alexander's "discovery" as the mark of an untutored essayist. Far more appropriate, to my mind, is the reading that seeks to account for the precise and forceful *untutorings* that these texts perform upon the essay, the reopening of possibility one might have thought foreclosed within expository prose.

In this sense the essays carry out on other terrain the central project of Alexander's poetics: the "leap" or "phase transition" addressed in Andrew Joron's afterword, the "spark" of new possibility Alexander speaks of locating in Aimé Césaire, Bob Kaufman, or Philip Lamantia. (This is a dialectics of the emergent new, not the mute agon of known oppositions.) A diasporan dialectics, then, or in Alexander's own inimitable phrase, thought carried on "the wing of imaginal African anti-gravity." To these locating instances for the essays, I might also add C. L. R. James's insistence on the primacy of living labor, for what such an insistence can help us to read of a way out of the postmodern doxology that valorizes a "materialist" poetics all too often by way of elevating word, utterance, syntax as alien *things* or subjectless *processes* over the "life-giving fire" of human creativity. (Materialism without full acknowledgement of the scope of living bodily, intellectual, and poetic labor simply collapses into matter. Posing an "otherwise" to this collapse is one of the crucial contributions of Alexander's writing.)

In selecting and arranging these texts for publication, I have been guided throughout by considerations of use to a general reader. Much important scholarship remains to be done on Alexander's multivalent and prolific body of work, and I hope that this volume will serve as a prompt for such work. For my part, I have tried to keep editorial intrusions to a minimum, relying for the most part on published versions of texts and Alexander's own typescript. Emendations have been undertaken sparingly in order to correct outright error, regularize certain idiosyncrasies of spelling, and in some cases to provide updated context for statements made more than a decade ago. In all cases, these changes have been made with the author's full involvement. I have also assembled the bare beginning of a citational apparatus for the work, but I pretend in no way that these endnotes are comprehensive. (Tracking in detail the scope and variety of Alexander's reading, and his determined re-tooling and inflection of cited text, would be a rewarding task for one of the hoped-for future scholars mentioned above).

Finally, rather than present a single linear chronology, I have chosen to arrange the texts in four thematic sections, followed by a final selection of interviews and a lecture. "The Magical Site Where the Future Must Convene" contains texts focused on the political geographies of community, globe, and points in between. "A Human Intensity" is devoted to monographs on individual writers, as well as homages, eulogies, and other texts with an individual focus. Texts in "The Wing of Imaginal African Anti-Gravity" are concerned with the poetics, cultural practice, and histories of the African diaspora. "A Relentless Meteoritics" is organized around Alexander's statements of poetics in its largest sense. The final section, "How One Speaks, How One Walks," presents three interviews and a lecture. Ordering within each section is chronological as far as the author and I could determine.

Far too many individuals to name provided editorial, material and moral support to the editor and author during the several years this project has been in preparation. Nonetheless, I would be remiss not to mention Andrew Joron, Garrett Caples, Sheila Scott-Wilkinson, Tanya Hollis, Tisa Bryant, and Joel Kuszai. My thanks to them, and most especially to Will Alexander.

TAYLOR BRADY / SAN FRANCISCO, 2008

THE MAGICAL SITE
WHERE THE FUTURE
MUST CONVENE

GEOGRAPHIES, HISTORIES, RESISTANCES

LOS ANGELES

THE EXPLOSIVE CIMMERIAN FISH

The American hour. Violence, excess, waste,
mercantilism, bluff, gregariousness, stupidity,
vulgarity, disorder. —AIMÉ CÉSAIRE

The planetary air now burns with transition, the russian bear is missing, the American Eagle, faulty, coughing up blood, after each of its foreign invasions. I'm speaking here of a tide washing the Western mental ethos bit by bit into an unremitting void, and the tide is dark, tropical, a-linear, African.

Because we exist in an era of intensive time acceleration, decades have been compressed into years, and years into months, and months into days. One can witness in present humanity a force analogous to geological surgeries taking place without letup. Not over 20 days after the Los Angeles ozone was blackened, the same energy infuses Bangkok, then the resignations of Daryl Gates and Prime Minister Suchinda transpire, symbolically and concretely representing the end of the corrupted pleiosaur's advantage. To paraphrase Césaire, leaders can no longer voluptuously wallow in "clichés," self-consumed in dispensable rhetorics. There is no time left for camouflage, for testimonials beclouded in deception. No, there is an inevitability at hand, a nervous taking of stock, as the "Southern" cone seeks to shake itself free of the "Northern" cone's monological reign over the dialectics of terrestrial existence. Shaking free of its deadly cuisines, its wholesale marketing of innocent blood for monetary gain and prestige.

Los Angeles, an explosive Cimmerian fish, has engendered insurgent anomalous fumes, as though spawned from fires in darkened Devonian waters. Fumes, more akin to lightning with its tense peripheral spillage, rising and ironically lighting those magnetic Goyaesque perils, those frontiers of stored up interior wrath, where destiny is focused by a seemingly mercurial vengeance, exploding the system of Imperial nerve vents. And these nerve vents have always mechanically palpitated at the whim of a racist, plutocratic aristocracy.

And the authorities of the land now clearly seen in the light of a ruthless psychic impoverishment, paralyzed in the agonizing throes of statistical explanation and panic.

Conversely, each of the dispossessed suddenly startled by the spontaneous current of articulate aphasia, have responded like the rapid heartbeat of an eagle silently salivating before tearing the flesh from its prey, the dispossessed suddenly slashing through the barbarian stereotypes so rampantly reinforced by the media as a given. The oppressed, the outraged, without warning, standing like magical lightning bolts, like boiling arithmetical titans, their uncanny stumbling quickly focused and sinister, guided by the forces of exponential resurrection.

This latter defiance seems at the root of the Los Angeles insurrection. I viewed the post trial interview with Lawrence Powell in a xerox shop filled with bibles at Manchester and Vermont hours before it burned into cinders. And an older Black gentleman, scriptures in hand, came up to me as I watched the officers' smug jubilation, and emotionally called for a balancing act by blood. I then stepped from the store into the street and immediately noticed that the people were galvanic with telepathy. And they understood their resurrection as coming from the passionate concentration of flame.

The King decision, like a reddish flare brutishly thrust in a wound, brought the colonial atmosphere to a pitch, and caused us as Blacks to vent a necessitous gangrene, bringing us in contact with the temperature of Indian animosity when forced to ingest the initial volleys of European acquisition and greed. This American enclave, initially garnered, and remains acquitted by the surgical implementation of homicide, in the main reserved for peoples of color, who collectively wake every dawn to intolerable rays of imposed barbarity and fatigue, with insults constantly branded upon grafts of our subconscious skin.

Having spent my earlier and later youth in the zones of both Los Angeles rebellions, I've come to understand the basic currency of anguish passed back and forth between the drowned and the drowned, whose reality fails to register upon the moguls of the daily Wall Street Exchange Indexes. And to what Dan Quayle refers to as the "average American," we Blacks are no more than annoying poltergeists. We remain to the majority occult, raging, maniacal, not to be trusted, looked upon as a criminal detour in genetic evolvement. So, to effect methodic insertion into this less and less viable mainstream, as persons of color, we must cover our core with a hideous salt so as to mime a Euro-American competence, in keeping with a behavioral duplicity and numbing, and by straining towards such a position, we are verbally forced to eschew the surreptitious evil which institutionally lurks in the cells of the body politic.

In contrast, I think of the 100,000,000 slaves murdered amidst the slime of the Middle Passage, animated by moans, and fever, and dying. Then there exists the sulfurous galaxy of continuing Indian murder and displacement, and here you have a national ambiance shaped at its core by insidious disharmony and greed. It is like an ocean of scars washing onto a shore of surcease and psycho-physical incarceration.

America, an incessant nitroglycerine story, where the sun has been historically stored to energize the crops of the ambassadorial slavers, crops, initially grown and watered by the blood of free labor. But during the revolt, a Rubicon has been crossed, and we have witnessed the tele-pathic artistry of revenge, the molecules of rebellion, which, because of optimum social deterioration, have exploded into a metamorphosis of nightmares, where wicker stick thrones have blown up and vanished.

The daily paper registers decline, as though witnessing the throes of the Roman population watching the year tragically darken, and turn into the continuing constriction of 455 A.D. All attempts at revival no more than impregnation and birth by a mother whose belly has been asphyx-iated by stone. We people of color are the barbarians sweeping into Rome from Asia and Gaul. Because of our insidious numbers we are inflicting genetic punish-ment upon the majority population. And here I speak not from emotion, but from a sense of inevitability. The masses, before an-other century closes will be composed of Egyptian yellow-brown. The key here is that the current majority cannot finance or murder its way out of the circumstance of a shrinking genetic base. As I see it, a quite palpable karmic backlash.

So I ask, where is the Belgian Congo, or German East Africa, or the Italian domination of Libya? Vanished, mesmerized by their continuing invalidation and disappearance. And so we turn to Herr Hitler with his thousand year boast, and Mussolini, and the anti-Semitic Stalin, astrally shaking in their grave boots, assaulted by the billion hallucinations of organic infinity. In keeping with these triune annihilations, there has been a contagious erosion of each Imperial attempt at colonial hegemony, the most accessible examples being the ferocious Algerian independence, and the double cyanide of Viet Nam to both the Americans and the French.

As for me, I've returned to the fevers of Moroccan trance intensity, to the aleatoric meters of the distant shaman's bell, calling me like a bird to the supreme longevity of the bluish outer stars shining in super-luminal immensity, "where communication is established with the higher states of being."[1] A communication so essential to my genetic lineage in the darker southern climes, where the rituals burn, where morality is electric. More simply put, I am seeking return to this original psychic reflex, with its mandibles charged by the alchemy of poetic smoke and catharsis.

Such communion is an energy which, by its very motion, desecrates the hobbled western legal codes, which have always deformed the rights of the collective darker races, which have tragically acquitted those who have bludgeoned in the name of racial subjugation, which have raised to levels of honor murderers, oily capitalizers, those who have horrifically infected the general health of the darker peoples with thumbnail germs scattered across the pages of their fetid legal amalgams. A legacy of cruelty, mendacity, and baseness. A legacy which has "no qualms about corpses."

Therefore, I align myself with the energies inherent in the wild specific-ity of Brazilian Indians, with the natural ambulations of tarantulas and Caimans, with the nomos of carnivorous Amazonian greenery, with its fire-ants stored in Cecropia trees, with its restless Jaguars and lizards, with its monstrous Acrosoma spiders. Here I am gliding down jagged rapids of sound, clothed with the decorative Peperomia leaves seismically watching the sub-conscious weathers of my brethren, as a former slave society, striking back at degradation, with the anger and force of a partially mutilated piranha.

A GALLERY COEXISTENT WITH INSPIRATION

We think of galleries as sprawled, as being rife with enfettered opinion, with an exclusive penchant for marketable canons. The painting is then imprisoned and only allowed to respirate at a sustained level of financial quantity, its impalpable powers simply noted as passing fact, or at best as exotic embellishment, in order to upgrade its virtues thereby giving it a higher monetary value.

It is the diametric of such thinking which maintains the ethic at the Gallery Tanner. It was opened in Los Angeles near the end of the 1970's, "when there were few venues for Black artists to display" their imaginal activity. Named after the Black expatriate artist Henry Ossawa Tanner, it is a physically condensed space not de-energized by the insidious prestige which accrues from high walls and square footage. One of its values lies in its intimate scope, which organically helps reduce the monolithic tension between the work of art and its public.

Its catalyst, Joyce Thigpen, "has put an emphasis on making the gallery accessible to . . . all income ranges" making it possible to ambulate the Tanner with one's focus concentrated upon the veracity of the work without having to reconnoiter a carking pecuniary dagger. When one leaves the glare of the boulevard one optically adjusts as if entering a realm charismatic with sensitivity. Because pretensions are voided the habitat brims by means of an ensconced balletic grace.

The patron is encouraged to intuitively probe, to ask questions seemingly out of range. The "advice to buyers" being "to get what you like first, then think about a possible return on your investment." Thus the ballistic challenge of all surface agenda is averted, then the scintillation of hues, the urgency of line, the balance of shape, becomes of paramount importance.

This is not to say that the gallery is flooded with works of inspired neophytes. The Tanner exhibits such artists as Romare Bearden, Jacob Lawrence, Elizabeth Catlett, and Alonzo Davis. And by perusing this short list we see the highest quality exerted, the judgment being such that externals are stripped, and fetid glossaries exploded. Rather than cold theatrical decorum, there is depth, rather than a glossed amnesial optics, there is clarity.

When walking into the Tanner, one gets the sense that the aboriginal is allowed to breathe, is allowed to live in its immaculate innocence, where a magic interplay transpires between the interior power of both viewer and creator. A living current, a transmogrified electrics. One then is suffused in a beatific enclave where creation can interact at the kinetic level of the uncanny. The inner motif of the work is allowed its intuitive vivacity.

Could one say that one enters into an intensity of recognition, as one would, say, encounter upon witnessing the unsigned renderings in the caves at Ayers Rock, or perusing the dazzling forms on the walls at Al-

<u>squill</u>   \ˈskwil\
noun

1a : a Mediterranean bulbous herb
(Urginea maritima) of the lily
family — called also SEA ONION —
compare "red squill"
1b : the dried sliced scales of a
squill used as an expectorant,
cardiac stimulant, and diuretic
2 : scilla

Middle English, from Anglo-French
squille, Lat. Squilla, scilla from
Gk. skilla [useless information]

consider May, late May, warm
    rain falling into blue squills

When I first heard ~~that~~ line,*
half asleep, I imagined squills
to be a coil shape, a swirl, a
    whorl, a whirl: onomatopoeia, →

* consider April, early April, wet snow falling into blue squills

But no, in the end, it's just
  another plant. — Comforting,
somehow, to know that: the way
it all of a sudden no longer
sticks out from its surroundings

          a bushel and a peck
                    Kit

timera? I cannot completely negate such a parallel, although the artists exhibited are known, the paintings and sculptings rendered by title. Again, in the Tanner's space the unblemished is allowed to breathe, the pure image allowed to jut forth, with commercial sophistry and its emblems confronted by ciphers, astringent with nullification.

[*The Tanner is no longer in operation*]

A SMALL
BALLETIC HIVE

The assumed results of creative workshops remain tangible objects: drawings, paintings, poems, small sculptings. A mono probing of the particular mediums pursued, honing their exterior state to a competent level so as to withstand a certain technical scrutiny. A creation externally fortified against palpable leakage, against standard incompetence.

To take writing as example: texts read, choices of phrasing discussed, fleeting forays into possible forms of publication. But to me such activity seems induced by a conservative pragmatics; a finished product no matter the consequence of the entropy that it faces in the long run. What I was concerned with in all three incarnations of my workshop was the praxis of the interior life.

First of all a state of mind must exist in order for any created form to appear. I introduced during the first five sessions the absolute need for inner fertilization. Not a dogmatic fertilization, but a need for embarking upon a quest for understanding the natural atmosphere of one's mind. Its predilection towards fire or quiescence, or its condition being of a curiously formed hybrid. The text consulted most useful in this regard was Edward de Bono's *Lateral Thinking*. A book of seminal exercises which allows thinking to go beyond selection and "open up other pathways,"[1] generating "as many alternative approaches as one can." Even after a promising direction has been found, other approaches should never be abandoned. Normally students are lauded for expertise in mastering a single limitation, but what was encouraged in this context was the relevance of movement for the sake of movement. To "change one's ideas," to generate flux even if that entails a kind of ambivalence or perception of incompleteness. Which recalls Surrealism's shattering of the sequential. As de Bono states, "the parts do not have to be self-supporting at every stage," so the whole idea of a proper or accessible manner of creating something is no longer upper-most in carrying a workable export into the world. Leaps can be made. One can start at G, work back to F, and eliminate A. I call it flexible ambulation through one's mental catacombs.

By engaging in such praxis the creative person begins to evolve a necessary discrimination, thereby understanding the isolation concomitant with one's imaginal efforts and the fickle circumstance of the public appraisal of those efforts. In keeping with this tenor we then began to probe the predatory nature of the marketplace. And at that point two seminal figures appeared in our purview: Joan Miró and Fernando Pessoa. The former's letters were quite revealing in this regard. His disdain for the thought of the provinces and their alignment with imaginal conformity. Then the legacy of Pessoa's imaginal flight in an indifferent Lisbon, creating his host of heteronyms, bringing to Portuguese a renown it had failed to know since the creations of Camoëns.

These examples among others brought to our small collective the eruptive point of character and the seminal power it embodies. By stressing character throughout our gatherings we would discuss the different texts perused always with an eye to the different personal approaches gathered. Normally we would range in number between five and ten souls, but the atmosphere seemed always capable of an electric plasticity generated from one of my random verbal sparks, which seemed to allow verbal cross-feeding, which would further inculcate co-nundrums. And this was good, because not only were there poets and writers present, but a Khlebnikov scholar, a former concert pianist, vi-sual artists, editors of film, all focusing upon the art of creativity. So in keeping with such a human array painters like Varo and Vlaminck, the aforementioned Miró, Matta and Matisse, were all discussed, as well as poetic mathematicians, such as Kurt Gödel and Georg Cantor. Then of course poets, such as Bob Kaufman, Blanca Varela, André Breton, Roger Gilbert-Lecomte, Philip Lamantia, Octavio Paz and Garcia Lorca were discussed.

After the first phase, which was entitled Psychic Fiesta, we entered the second phase, which was entitled Passion & Ethics. It centered around the theme of self-challenge and the interior nucleus of courage which was understood to flow as an essential plasma. One could say that a vivacity of understanding and resistance began to evolve from the readings and the exchanges, and so the organics of poetic collectives were discussed under present world conditions on week eight of Passion & Ethics. Then the question was put, "Should current institutions be at-tacked, or should they be left to meander and die?" It seemed the latter gained a more favorable reading. In 1964, André Breton said that we were entering a "neutral zone," and the shapes which Surrealism took during its incipient phases were no longer applicable. Which led to for-ays into quantum physics relating its nonsequential character to the present imaginal field and the imperceptible shift into more refined zones of awareness. More refined arrays of assault on the current tem-poral forces, like an electrical contagion which slowly takes over a body.

One thing was agreed upon, that the era which followed the Second World War has entered an irreversible Waterloo. And it was agreed that the century itself, for all intents and purposes, drew to a close at the fall of the Berlin Wall. The feeling was such that the world population had entered a liminal zone, called by the Maya the "nameless days," which "were considered unfortunate . . ." These were the five empty days of the Mayan solar calendar where beings took refuge from the world. Paraphrasing this period, one could call it the five empty days of poison, where confusion and danger existed as principal hallmarks. This being understood as a prevailing general condition, we convened upon the third phase of the workshop entitled Interiority & Light. Texts from René Guénon, Henry Corbin, and Ananda Coomaraswamy became dominant. An attempt to return to one's inner power, not in terms of some didactic religiosity, but opening up the fecund chemistry of one's creative ducts.

This is not to say that individual works were not read and critiqued, nor an isolated reverie brought to scale over the power necessitous in works. We did exercise in our small balletic hive.

The idea of the workshop was to draw from the being powers which were buried, outward, so as to actively attack imaginal complacency. And in this regard Juan Goytisolo was a shining example. When the great Spaniard attacked his former incarnation as a didactically hallowed prince of Communist right thinking, he exhibited the courage to extinguish his narrowed agenda, his airtight Marxist programmatics, thereby forgoing superficial adulation in order to swell within the imaginal kingdom of true fertility and chance. A writer no longer of the enterprise to command the range of an infertile public. By working with such examples as this, we began to brew a creative fuel capable of transmuting collective biography.

IGNITING THE
INWARD PRODIGY

Since the watermark of the Cartesian, meaningful thought has been construed as moving "in a clearly defined direction" toward a clearly incontestable outcome. Such structuring of the mind puts supreme concentration upon selective thinking, which proceeds sequentially, moving step by each justifying step. We see this, and the resulting codification, in most aspects of our day-to-day living, especially in education, in standardized student testing. All goals are recognizable, all progressions accounted for. It is like addition by abacus: each thought is a "digit in its appropriate column."

The mind most treasured in this world is the one that brilliantly complies with the strenuous complication of the unadorned result. Of course, this is the left hemisphere of the brain working at its optimum. In such a climate, the discontinuous is viewed with perpetual suspicion, and those minds lacking the same measurable fluency are marked as having an ignominious intelligence.

At the beginning of my educational sojourn, I was marked by this lessening. I know firsthand that this marking causes pain to the self and that this pain inhibits the power beginning to accrue in one's being. By age seven, I already felt as if I had failed to secure stability in this life. I had not developed the tools to join the established reading collective, to interpret written characters, and to gain sense from their arrangement. So I was banished to the lowest rung of that collective. To compensate, I engaged in imaginative forays. I turned great fig trees into winged vertical blueness, I imagined ancient sienna cities that I would arrange from stones that I'd find, and I modeled cinnabar ponies from mud. These inner flights helped me reconnoiter the shadows of fear. I could say that in this, my first poetic experience, I was intuitively understanding the rudiments of Edward de Bono's "lateral" world, much in advance of his findings. This is not to say that a seven-year-old had evolved any trenchant understanding of the anti-linear as technique. But I knew my indwelling grasp by touch, solitude, and the inner dialectic, which formed my basic principle of balance. Thanks to the diligence of one concerned instructor, a Mr. Beacon as I recall, the character began to coalesce to such a degree that the print became comprehensible enough that I was able to work at an "acceptable minimum." Reading is a practical necessity: it allows one to gain a working into this world and also the capacity to counter its tenacious reasoning. It was a skill that ultimately allowed me to illuminate my inner complexity by engaging me in subjects as disparate as botany and poetics.

I am not presenting myself as a singular case. There are many others like me. As a writing instructor, I am always looking to restructure the classroom. "Advice," "restrictions," and "explanations" no longer subsist as guiding forces. What I seek to create is a hive of tactile opportunity, what I call "verbal painting." For instance, I take the noun *bird* and then ask the students what a bird does. Immediately hands go in the air. From there we get into colors, types of birds, patterns of flight, the difference between sea birds and land birds, types of food consumed, night birds, day birds, birds that fly, birds that walk over land. We delve into geography, diet, animal behavior, and astronomy. Rather than a sterile topography of facts, this creates a scent, an inner motivation to encounter worlds that students never knew existed. The students become immediately involved.

The only way knowledge becomes an inspiring element in one's life is through a lifelong motivation that outstrips diplomas and titles. As catalyst/instructor, my objective is to allow the students' interior presence to emerge without the facts being a restrictive force. This is how curiosity exudes so that student and instructor can meet in an existential mean, and all the facts from the instructor fall on fertile aural scapes, allowing unforeseen growth to transpire.

I have found this type of approach fruitful to a vast array of communities—from challenged fifteen-year-olds in south central Los Angeles to poets and writers five times their age in the comfortable setting of Hofstra University on Long Island. Whether the student is fifteen or seventy-five, of whatever ethnicity, the issue is to find out what motivates him or her so that an inward sparking takes place and dialogue is established. This dialogue needs to be more than simply between student and instructor in the classroom. It needs to be an ongoing connection for the student, so that an unmonitored arousal takes place in his or her being.

It is vital that the catalyst/instructor be most concerned with the individuals he or she is communing with. Not only at the college or university teaching levels is this essential, but also at those interesting levels where the fifteen- or eighteen-year-old has not evolved beyond the basic rudiments of reading. This is where the "Eastern"—or more particularly, African—model comes into play for me. According to traditional African values, "the person preexists and by incarnating himself . . . seeks to open himself, to grow, to insert himself always more effectively" into the larger society. The person is central in this context—not the institution, as in the West.

With these ideas in mind, I bring prints or paintings to class as a stimulus to writing. The students are excited not only by subject matter and color, but also by the artists' biographies. Miró is a perfect example. What I stress when discussing him is the purity of his creative character, a character infused with anxiety, transmutation, and discipline. While speaking to the students about how to achieve balance in a poem, I use *The Farmer's Wife*, one of Miró's early paintings. Why this painting rather than a later painting from his oeuvre? Because I instinctively learned from this painting the art of verbal equilibrium. How the weight, the coloration, and the alchemical linkage of each word creates an unerring magic. I tell the students what Miró said concerning *The Farmer's Wife*—that he had made the "cat too large," throwing "the picture out of balance." He went on to say that this was "the reason for the double circles and the two angular lines in the foreground" of the painting. From this visual example I introduce the idea of interior sonority. How, in the magic of a poem, tables, stars, and rivers can blend as immaculate homonyms.

During a recent class at the Naropa Institute, I made up a random list of words ranging from *ice* to *fire*, from *Ecuador* to *pyramid*, from *hummingbird* to *gold*. I then asked each student to connect these particles electrically. The results were singular and each piece carried its own particular coloration. What I was stressing was not some predetermined motion, but a response that charged each composition—electricity being the difference between quotidian and poetic levels of language. Creation needs to continuously germinate in the mind of the reader, listener and

viewer. This is what Antonin Artaud once termed the "electrical revolution," the transmuting of electricity by means of spontaneous resonance.

Working over the past three years with Theater of Hearts/Youth First,
a non-profit Los Angeles-based arts organization, I have encountered
students who have been abandoned and forgotten by the conventional
institutions of learning. These are young people who have been detained
by law, who are transitioning into the challenges of schooling after recent incarceration. For them, the great Afro-Cuban painter Wifredo Lam
is an inspiring example. Lam made groundbreaking work engendered
by his African heritage. I show them how he lit the volcano of Orishas in
painting his symphonic trance called *The Jungle*. Lam commenced work
on *The Jungle* in 1942, and from its beginning it was a magnetic sum of
his imaginative powers. I use the painting as an example of artistic
courage, the courage to express who you really are.

In Lam's own words, *The Jungle* "was intended to communicate a psychic state." After all, Cuba is not a land of jungles. This painting is therefore a prime example of trusting one's own interior cosmology. I tell students to think of the shapes and colors as words, as if the picture were a
splendiferous verbal anatomy. Seeing the audacity of Lam's painting
gives a kind of license to these nouveau verbal practitioners. It lets them
know that one does not use conventional means to express artistic
power. I tell them that to create and sustain power, one must study one's
medium with an inward patience in order to raise one's writing to a level
of perpetual quality. This turns their concentration toward the interior
state, in this sense transmuting the negatives of their former street activity into the seminal activity of language. Working from this state of
mind, they produce stunning writing. Being exposed to great artists,

whose backgrounds at times echo their own, inspires them to meet life's challenges with another form of lightning in their eye.

We are educating people, not numbers. The most important thing is to understand that each individual is capable of providing unique insights into the subject at hand. I always try to employ de Bono's concept of "suspended judgment," which allows the possibility for increasing new, seemingly curious approaches. Not that all approaches will prove significant in the end, but in their sum they generate motion, which in turn generates further motion. What takes place in such a conclave are unforeseen outlooks which help to draw out hidden powers from the subject at hand. It's like moving around a seemingly stationary chandelier, seeing at one angle blue-green, at another orange-red, at yet another lilac or ocher. The combinations proliferate. The effect of these combinations may not occur until three weeks after working with a group in this mode of free exchange, but even so, a tacit understanding begins to make itself felt. As David Bohm has so artfully stated, "If we are communicating at the tacit level, then maybe thought is changing." It is the duty of the catalyst/instructor to stir up the life force in all students, the seventy-year-old as well as the fifteen-year-old, so that inner circulation is activated. Even if it is for a fleeting moment that they see a wider possibility, it is the first opening to a freedom that soars beyond the harried routine of debility.

A NOTE ON THE GHOST DIMENSION

TO ANDREW JORON

The void exists in the illusive dunes of Afghanistan. These upper relics of ghosts charged with the most ferocious diplopia. The mind of the American soldier as if eight months out on Mars, void of provincial guidance, his god refusing to appear, each day and night a poisonous cinnabar smoke. Waking and sleeping amidst the language of the asteroids. So when retaliation prevails the summit of the human bodily field becomes no more than active participation by dread. And we see the contagion of this dread suffused inside the office worker, the wary circus matron, listless and uninspired by collapse. In keeping with this collapse I think of deadly heat as the intangible core of our present, living as it does by means of a despicable neutron thesis. Burn your hand, catch your arm in fire, and you feel the central force of overwhelming destruction. But to provoke that destruction by a stunted and inclement thinking is merely rife with plutonic value. Can we migrate to the asteroids? Does Titan at present represent a habitable enclave? Of course all answers occupy the zone of negation. To silence speech, to condemn the human species to suicide—language will never allow this. And language as we know it is this elliptical alchemical ether with moons flowing in its pho-nemes. Nineteen-thirty-nine a relic in this regard. Pearl Harbor a hor-rific but accessible rigidity. So living by means of poetic insight as sensi-tivity I live every day by the continuing emphasis of apartheid. As Baraka once put it ". . . the sensitive collect and carry." A fallout from the inaugu-ral racism of the empire. There exist the haunted Indians in Guatemala, squalid pockets of suffering in Asia, where people feed on the absence of gruel. There exist the aboriginals ransacked in North America, the con-tinent of Africa, robbed and parched of its original inspiration. Now, the twin towers and their ongoing aftermath, with the burning glass, and bodies falling through the air to secular burial grounds of dread. But by adherence to unilateral attack America opens itself up to the powers of the fumes of retaliatory ghosts. If all the orchards go astray and burn what will rescue us from Andromeda? If the oceans turn a green Venu-sian liquid what will survive? Statistics no longer thrive. Popular astrol-ogy is misleading. Yet the five empty days on the calendar of the Maya persist in my vision. Days when monsters appeared, when nights re-versed and people hovered in a poisonous neutrality. Let's say it like this. Our bodies are invisible documents because our language continues tracing those other stellar locales where we invisibly glide to other galac-tic possibilities far beyond the suicidal repartee which the American tenor so fitfully engages. In twenty billion years a new sun will be form-ing, with green light burning beyond human debate. Only a vatic recita-tion can overcome rehearsals for destruction.

TO THE BLOODLESS REFUGEES OF EMPTINESS

Through the suburbs sleepless people stagger,
as though just delivered from a shipwreck
of blood. —GARCIA LORCA, "The Dawn"

What now exists as palpable global destiny? What are its markers, its sculpted crimson signs?

The psychic atmosphere implies a return to troubled fiefdoms, to monarchies trebled by ferocious glints of bloody erosion. The Sun continues to burn, the tides swarm across the shores with their sulphurs, while human continuity appears and disappears, like a nettling grimness of ghosts. What arises from this startling anti-mass is the progressive neutering of the species. During this continuing dearth of higher foci even lightning is misconstrued as mere electrical theatrics. World citizenry now progresses as an artificial epitaph, as a spotted hyena starving on kelp, in an atmosphere of plight, hovering in balanced enigma. A spoiled voltage, a principle lacking in cohesion, where horizons disintegrate, where ideographs explode into darkness.

Humanity, like generic refugees, profanely strewn across a dome of exploded heliographs. The politicians crave for momentary incisions, for influential poison, much like staggered antelopes searching for sublime direction. For instance, a once dependable compass, now a locust eaten crystal. The collective path, a roving generation of hatchlings, devolving in sullen mental savannahs. We've witnessed many centuries of émigrés, of disruptive holocaust phantoms. Now, all the fiestas and deities somatically crippled, maundering like leaves across sudden hurricane waters, with their destinies entangled in a liminal brushfire pyroclastic.

At present, the shadow of our phylum wafting through an unremitting mime osmotics. The linear goal, the abstracted referent, now remains increasingly hidden in tumultuous occlusion. And what is engendered by the latter, is the bloodless wake for unidirectional propaganda.

After all the rancid colonial murders, after all the wrenching cortical spills, after falsified wars between Saxon systems and anti-systems, we have come to intolerable deficits, howling with negated stochastics. The embrangled heads of state implanting pyres on the death shores, accruing impasse models, sickened hybrid potions. The inner cuisine at present exists as a phrenic lake where poison fish are eaten. The bones are then dissected by mental nomad rifles, by bizarre involuntary lexical slaughter. What increasingly subsists is a ruthless fatality of emptiness, mistaken risk having crossed into the zone of "the hereafter."

What now occurs in the West are circumstantial remnants, listless mastications, like a metropolis of haunted rivets, exchanging commands through a violent anorexia. Acuity now transpires within a blank and enervated interval. All the emotions are mimicked as though there existed a belief, a magnetic resin which once found succor in the decisive cir-

cumstantials of a Kutosov or a Patton. Since the ramparts no longer dazzle, how can the use of blades defend against shadows? We've come to the
bickering of monads, which expire and resurrect on a scope, soaked in a
bloodless skeletal haze. Moments are now defined by sussurant equivo-
cal rotation, by kinetics poised beside the lamp of surcease. The general
mood, reflexive, at penultimate extremis in limbo.

This anxiety goes back to the dawn of the 1440's with the European
quest for foreign acquisition, for external perfection, with the Northern
integument given outranking status. Human quality was put under
siege, and in the Southern climates this quality became a radical sorcery
to be brutally subdued. Then this latter world was divided into seas and
enclaves, by the Portuguese, the Spanish, the Dutch, the English. This resulted in the successive exterminations of peoples of color over the span
of the five following centuries. And from the fruits of this labor there has
come to exist a general epic of nothingness. A hallucinogenic baseness,
surrounded by a strange day to day quotidian disruption. The human
physiology now languishing in a gulf, its dynamical particulars inten-
sively seized with increasing strength from the forces of extinction. As if
forces of bacteria had opened themselves to an unconfined momentum,
explorational in their horror.

What presently smolders is a desperate search for mathematical
shamans to repopulate expression with reassuring rigidity, so as to give
the functioning of matter the static procedure of paradise. Because the
eucharist is now a phlegm-wracked body, tainted by opium and murder.
The color of its eyes has revealed the wrangling scent of bestial enerva-
tion. In the zones of Manhattan, in the pyretical confines of The City of
The Angels, live wayward populations, performing as in a staggered ballet of estranged and exploded spiders. Their dialogue scattered between

immolation and leakage, with its recent heritage clustered around the old Nagasakian chronicles, the dense memoirs of the Solzhenitsyn gulags, the Hitlerian propositions conjoined by x-rays and voltage.

Such is the cruelty we currently inhabit, distorted as transitional bipeds, with our tenuous salvo of ethics, disastrously routed along fractures of separation and antimony.

Leadership is now called for directed along the lines of a Nepalese thought practitioner. Persons, whose dynamical gifts rise above emptied chariots whose hydrogen has gone bad. Such oblique leaders are capable of transmuting action from the catacombs of ruin, with a wise and circular gospel of magic. Such are the leaders of a true alchemical amnesty.

When the vertical disciplines were slaughtered, such insight was destroyed. Now it attempts to rise once more above the shadows of material fallacy. Such are the beings who've magically held the human zone intact throughout a series of phantom standoffs with nothingness. To picture these great magicians of the cells, one will have to forgo the personality as seen from outward directional gathering, with its poisoned myth of status. An image cleansed of particulates, of measurable tyrannical denseness, yet charged with the jottings of a new transitional body. And from such daring evolvement, an enriched new genus of blankness registers beyond the old a-tonic canonical eras, as they've been plotted within a maze, and governed by the harsh enclitics of reason. Yes, bold neoteric practitioners, like dark amphibians rising into anti-carnivorous lunations, casting vibrations by means of invisible greenness, which magically mix the visible measure with the post-mortem helix. Such is the carrier of vertical phasmas, of the prototype of drift. Then the summons to runic green bastions, to heights of philosophical eaglets, with conduct ceasing to flare as outer fragmentary poise. From this, wisdom becomes circuitously increscent, as from the blazing root of ghosts, they who transmute the glyphs from anti-turpentine monarchs, so that each remarkable act is taken as a sigil, the aforementioned nothingness, discussed as indecisive homage, verbally coined in Greek and liminal vulture.

Within the deadly waters of the Western temporal end, such utopian balletics are seemingly endowed with cryptographic fatigue, yet inscrutably kindled by a telepathic ozone. This latter being the essence which hones the galaxies to a pitch of internal luminosity. A utopia which thrives throughout transitional suspension, with its voice of vicarious crystal extending and retreating, between eternity and terra firma, so that there exist the cryptic motif, the transpersonal scarab, comprising an index of hierarchical edicts.

In Nepal, such conveyance is the natural praxis of the "guruva," capable of bringing forth life out of death. Saying such, I am thinking of the magical puja ceremony, by which the great Bengal tiger is conjured out of emptiness. Not "pointless agitation," but impalpable power operant at a piercing transparency, absolutely nonaligned with "baseless fantasy" and error. Even in concerns mundane, the guruva is able to result, the purest concentration through the powers of anti-persona. Of course, this is seen by many moderns as pejorative, as obscene juggling of reality. But what concerns us here is the suprarational realia, the electrical unification, the rising above matter in its mode as dyslexic interval. The personality then taking on a life as transfunctional kinetic, uranian, and motionless as oration.

But the human structuring axis remains the Roman world model, pursued with poisonous momentum, like a negated Flavian centaur. A life which forcefully questions the riddle, which ignites by its disasters a prolonged and fragmentary gossip. This is not the circumstance we seek, with its scarred and despicable motives, its plainspoken gargantuan, lisping, now post-mortem in calumny, passed forward blindly, into cold reductive laws and conclusions. Condoned magistrates, corrupted political leaders, are elected by surreptitious mandate, to fluctuate within the motion of their disabled missives. For instance, filth-ridden judgments against the principled use of homeopathic medicinals, against enforced financial sanctions for the tribe of the powerful, with their obscenely wealthy cohorts, strutting through electrically decorative corridors, empowered by the genes of voracious hyenas. Then one arrives at the barrier of broken social mobility, where the destitute unrelentingly peer, into a profane focus, into the illusive and trans-sonic reason of the general political dialectic.

For the common constituent, this means the confused rapidity of individual opinion, momentarily accepted as prevailing mental logic, the voter as such, swayed by a virulent and transitory "verbalism," the politician aggressively sculpting a partisan priority, attempting to evolve a fate, which, on the night of election will become the victorious voice of official pronouncement. The press will announce the candidate's personal apogee, which will one day be chronicled in accord with lifeless memorials. This, the glossary of an encompassing mundane, with its chronic flaws, with its institutional hepatitis. The commentators chattering like plutonic egrets, mimicking their own flight in reversal. A circumstance conditioned to a prime complicity with the tragedy of a hateful criteria, as competition proceeds by means of flameless radium farming.

These are the seizures by which the postcolonial is staggered. The Western vulgus now invaded by a rhymeless desiccated wandering through a maze of sunless hectographs, thirsting for amazement or fever. Yet the masses remain annulled, looking for brutish approval, or reclaiming their worth around a fractious allegiance to some cold ancestral murdering well. The social cells consumed by assault form habitual rivalry. Thus, true insight is shattered, real living is averted.

In contradistinction, the Nepalese guruva, calling through preternatural rites, to kindle electrical stars in the blood, by having contingents of people break apart and drift, and regather by telepathy. This, the true arcane, the life above vulcanian zones. It is the orbit where the bodiless is trusted, where the proto-solar living world exists, as a sacred electrical drama, as a codex of fire, as a magical agamas of roses.

AGAINST THE STATE AND ITS FUTURE AS A HOMICIDAL ENCLAVE

> *... This flagrant negation of humanity which constitutes the very essence of the State is, from the standpoint of the State, its supreme duty and its greatest virtue ... This explains why the entire history of ancient and modern states is merely a series of revolting crimes; why kings and ministers, past and present, of all times and all countries—statesmen, diplomats, bureaucrats, and warriors—if judged from the standpoint of simple humanity and human justice, have a hundred, a thousand times over earned their sentence to hard labor or to the gallows.* —MIKHAIL BAKUNIN

At its core the state has characterized its praxis as ballet by liquidation, as an injudicious social strife, as a dark microbial ballast, its itinerary being the scalding dust measured by the clockwork of mayhem. Its memoirs, more in keeping with microscopic rubellas, with politically allotted viral infections. And each survivor of such besiegement is alphabetic with maiming, with shaken poltergeist's terror, condemning every wakeless succor with unobtainable ambrosia.

Take the Guatemalan plight of internally displaced peasants. The abortive auto-golpe during 1992 of President Jorge Serrano, which suspended the Supreme and Constitutional Courts, the offices of the Attorney General, and the Human Rights Procurator was reversed by "moderate sectors of the army," "popular organizations," and human rights opposition, forcing Serrano, and his Vice President Espina into exile, because leadership under their civilian grip remained rife with bloody torture, with extrajudicial executions. "Some victims were shot outright in the presence of witnesses; others were abducted," "then tortured and murdered." Take the execution of Luis Alvarez Concoa, a law student abducted in March of 1993, and his body found mutilated the following month. Or take the case of Tomás Lares Cipriano, "shot dead the day after organizing protests against the presence in his area of military and civil patrols." The former being but particles of a titanic and ghastly census.

Even after the new president assumed office the killing went unabated and flowed like bones into the sea. Under the newly installed de Leon "his cousin and . . . political ally was murdered, just weeks into his leadership." And this in no way takes into account the scandalous scuttling of rural body parts greedily ransacked by vultures. Other telling specifics could be drawn from the slaughters in East Timor, or ignescent decapitations so troubling in Rwanda, or the electric prods as condoned in Montevideo, or the juvenile executions of Curtis Harris and Ruben Cantu under the auspices of draconian Texas statutes.

On the surface there seem to exist varying degrees of heinousness, or drained liters of blood, yet what prevails in the state is an uncontestable arrhythmia, in league with a cruel and unusual controlling debility. One can enlarge upon heinous specifics, but general assessment attests to plasmic leakage in Guinea, in China, against the Indians in Chiapas. According to Webster's, a nation "is a stable historically developed community of people." Yet prevailing documents tell us that decay, erosion, the imploding policy of the inch-meal, has become the focused life of a foreseeable and menacing agenda.

One is not speaking of a code eclectic with ruses, or declinatory actions as to murder, but a fruitless and stabilized minority, like Suharto in Indonesia, or the chaotically elected PRI, with its gross succession of banditry. The questions must be asked, has the nation lost its cause? have its people been inevitably shredded into suicidal enclaves? One thinks of the rich being dangerously pampered on volcanic ice and rum, while the majority, like the scions in the Brazilian favelas, forced, to ignite their own bread over sulphur, and then ingest its infested pablum. A tableau which bespeaks of a generic implosion of ruin, of rotted limbs, of politically maneuvered viral fatigue, within a zone of relentless plutonics. The tribulation is global, Hitlerian, and the victims are seen as stunned and unlettered, at the core being nothing but expendable cartilage, sprawled across a comatose theatrics.

There is only so much longer that the aristocracy can bewilder, can neatly poison its own implements, before its previous centuries of cruelty begin to claustrophobically rot, and overtake its current power of immunity, staffed with anthrax maps, with roulette dice, with bloodied killing gages.

Take the blood ridden sleep of a butcher, how long can his dreams obscure the skulls of his victims, their incarnadine balletics, invigored with the daunting glow of a disfigured zebra. Yes, the repressed gustatory delicacy. Or the thrill of the quasi-governing Khmer Rouge, having human flesh torn whole by the insatiable edacity of crocodiles. This is statehood propelled by the cartography of murder, or positional stampede by injustice. Policy seems to scatter from one confine to another, but one can say bureaucracy by lizard, execution by trained piranha and their Myrmidons.

Not exaggeration or ridicule, or the psychological invariation of the neutralized chronicler trying to abstract depravity. But the blood, the human salt and bone is real. The preconcluded tribunals, both cowardly and obnoxious, with the detestable inveracity of a manged and weighted hyena. As Mikhail Bakunin so trenchantly put it, "The State is the organized authority, domination and power of the possessing classes over the masses ... the most flagrant, the most cynical, ... the most complete negation of humanity. It shatters the universal solidarity of all men on the earth, and brings some of them into association only for the purpose of destroying and conquering, and enslaving all the rest."[1]

So under these conditions how will the coming millennia transpire? What of the perjured campaigns, of the duplicitous vipers in coat tails?

It bodes of calamitous disappearance in blood, but for now it is all official business. The starvation lines, the smoke that swirls from the bayoneted bodies. So with this as backdrop has humanity been reduced to a legislated suicide? To a new amalgam of skuas, gluttonous with cancellation, dreaming while at rest of a collective globe of corpses? Asking such, how will the current interstice proceed, with its maniacally harried calm, with its reflexive predation condemned to transpire like a globally netted harem?

Each leader seems nothing more than a noxious quotidian androgyne, parading a list of velvet Imperial plaudits, not far different than the smoky reflections of Stalin, or the seeping avarice of Nero.

What results are constitutions within a foul and cyclical pestilence, within trajectories that are "bed fast," uncritical, insalubrious. There now exists a blighted transition of confused and imperious plebiscites, of pestiferous voting measures. As regards the individual, that is where the cunning dissolve, and genuine value accrues. This being the magical site where the future must convene. Not upon the premise of a habitual and incompetent treachery, but upon another trenchant co-option, such a person is called in the Afro-historical context, a maroon, a runaway. So if each state has its center within the realm of a corrupt inclemency, it is for these maroons, these dissidents, to rise and collect in a higher diversity, people now known as perpendicular Venezuelans, as disenchanted Ghanaians, as anti-imperial Americans, rising from the drone of state sponsored killing, with a consciousness radically shifted from horizontal paranoia to a praxis of edenic thresholds. The latter, corresponding to a nonbehaviorist reflex, to a vibrational bastion, embodied in Vindemiatrix, the "Yellow-white giant, 75 light years" away. It is a star which "can strengthen resolve and the ability to follow through where other individuals are involved." It can also "assist greatly in deeper modes of apprenticeship or learning between the individual and the group," particularly where what is being learned is not fully comprehended "at the outset."2 Of course one is not speaking of thought as fraudulence, or action insidiously prone to escapist enclosure, but life directed to a more congruous power, to a mode of non-murderous perceptual proclivity. The concern here being the reduction of callous mental stunting, the beginning dissolution of a factitious dread. From the perspective of the plunderer, this is no more than utopian frivolity, no more than empyreal naïveté.

But what is being advanced is a fresh neurological balance, like a fish which ceases to respirate in water and strikes out across a new impressive land bridge. The people's purposes transmuted, as to bravery, assault, and the monetary profits accruing from certain aspects of death.

Instead of engaging in elaborate requisitions of terror, human energy will more engage in instinctive apical concerns. Eventually this will lead to other living examples in the galaxy.

With this as the focus, the water supplies transfigured from rust, the systems of finance more angled with balance, with the social actions no longer drilled by a short set of charges. The ideal no longer marked by the voice of lugubrious profit.

To speak as such, does one solely strike aim at a comet? Or does one transcendentally seek refuge in the powers which infuse anonymous hurricanes and tsunamis?

One is simply rising above the tremors of panicked locales. It is like awakening from a dreaded hieroglyphic, no longer recognizing the confine one once saw at the beginning of one's soporific endeavor. Something new, as if for the first time taking in contents unperceived in one's former habitation. This is an inward flame, blue, and lit beyond the tide of patriotic killing. The recent Saxon governings no longer a creed to be copied, to negatively infect the postcolonials, be they in parts of Africa, or Paraguay. Let the British truly die with their African demarcations; let the French, with their monolinguistic salvos perish, with the strength of their own inconsequence. As for the Dutch and the current Americans, time will suddenly burn their arrogant radium trapezes; will scorch, and smolder, and irradiate their gains, with the lingering Roman nightmare, circa 581 A.D.

CURRENT EMPIRE AS NEMESIS

In the West for the past five hundred years, privileged parts of the human populace have favorably viewed themselves in mirrors of aristocratic insolence. From this perspective, exploration and colonization of the earth have seemed limitless, granted by God-given authority. But upon closer examination, the aforementioned legacy has left living activity perched closer and closer to an abyss from which no recovery seems possible. A collective implosion minus any buffer or rescue from any nearby galactic intelligence.

This implosion seemed to be spawned by "Old World" colonization which commenced in the 1480's, when the Portuguese, under Antonio Gon-salves and Nuno Tristan, brought back from Africa, with assistance from Prince Henry the Navigator, ten slaves as a present to Pope Martin V. And it is from this seed that animals as well as beings of darker integument have suffered under prolonged mephitic stewardship. A prelude of omens, most notable in the palpable demise of the current planetary climate.

It has been said that the Hudson River held so many fish, that during the 1600's the Indians simply scooped them from the waters by the basket full. Sea otters, walruses, dolphins, whales, blazed during this era with unlimited variety. Yet, within 150 years, between 1750 and 1900, all of the above "had been harvested to the brink of extinction." For instance, "Stellers sea cow . . . was nearly extinct a mere twenty years after its discovery." And it is this context which prevails in many quarters where "Wildlife housing" is seen as an annoying embranglement, unconnected to the greater priority of short term profit. One could occupy list after list of globalized ruination. "New England groundfishery" collapsed, "Northwest Pacific Salmon" struggling against reproductive oblivion. In South America, seagrasses dissolving, coral reefs "dead or endangered." The Black Sea fatigued by pollution. In East Africa, "non-sustainable" "blast fishing." In the South Pacific, threat from "coral mining." This negative loss of habitat is nothing that the media deems worthy of sustained perusal. Again, this psychology of colonization has been of constant stimulus to the spiraling destruction of life as we know it. These colonists of the mind always claim that they are the "harbinger of the superior order" and progress. But killing and plundering always travels in their wake. At first, the central victims were the "Indians," "the yellow peoples," the Blacks. Now it has spread to the ocean itself, which has become a pure policy of suicide. And I am not just thinking of the Black Sea and its "oxygen starved deserts," but a lethal planetary schema. It is acceptable to the progressive sensibility when Vietnam chronically suffers from land mines and shrapnel, when children starve in the Congo and Haiti, when Appalachia goes missing in the chronicles. For the above are considered to be nothing more than miserable lands and peoples never counted on the economic graphs, because they derive from unsuitable origin.

These are values which commingle in a concrete and inescapable smoke. A smoke as sworn enemy to any monetary redistribution. True, there exists the ease of goods and services in most parts of the West, but the long term cost seems inimical to collective survival. I say this because these aforementioned values have been exported to lands which can in no way sustain them. Even a populous giant like China seems to struggle under the weight of conflicting choices. A seeming ease on the eastern seaboard, but floods and famine in its provinces to the west. In addition, its eastern economy is responsible for the spillage of 7.6 metric tons of waste per year.

This is like constant injury going untreated. General immunity is weakened. If no care is significantly forthcoming one can begin to speak of serious threat to the injured organism's well being. This is a universal principle in nature. Superficially, what results from this condition is positive statistical ostentation, and a reverence for microscopic mechanics. Irradiated food harvests, global e-mail transmission. As final appendix to this note I must give voice to our interstellar alternatives. None of the following worlds with any aquatic reprieve.

Mars: waterless, feral with unlivable winds
Saturn: sidereal rotation of a decade
Jupiter: ubiquitous meteorology as violence
Neptune and Pluto: hellish cornucopias of darkness and ice Venus:
    boiling
Alpha Centauri: light years beyond human boundary

The above being our immediate alternatives to the trees that we kill, to the soils that we break.

We are faced with this nemesis of thought, in large part American, impelling psychic separation, always exporting signals which condone environmental hoarding. A punishment to living beings, always exposing us to dangerous cosmic isolation.

The current values at best can only lead to a more crippled humanity, to earth as a compost of maps, no more significant than the regolith founded upon the asteroid Egeria.

CHINA

MODERN ASPIRATION
AS MORASS

China, an oblique invehicular giant pulled, like a tightrope of tensors between the sophisticate forms of the marketplace, and its a-rational insuperable countryside. On the one hand, the furnace that is Shanghai, on the other, the palaces of straw in the outer provinces of dearth. The government now posed between these poles, between an abrasive proto-opulence, and the stony modicums of the peasants, is eaten by invincible insomnia, embargoed as it is by conceptual dictation concerning modernity and its springs, and its simultaneous ideology amassed along the lines of far-flung repression. It is a neutered typhoon with its scales of movement halted, struggling in contradictory surcease.

Take the Three Gorges Dam along the Yangtze River. According to the authorities and its main proponent Li Peng, it will "increase . . . affordable electricity . . . , control floods, boost the growing economy," reduce the pollution of air, and lessen China's impact on the ozone layer. But contradicting this practical impact will be the forced resettlement of 1.4 million people, "the submerging of ancient farmland," the burial of wildlife habitats and temples, along with archaeological gold teeming back in the past some 10,000 years.

Will its construction remain adamant over eons, or will its final result supersede the tragedy of Henan province, when typhoons struck its titanic 62 dams unleashing a demonic dragon of water, erasing whole enclaves, killing a quarter million people, keeping other millions trapped in disease and simultaneously tied to an aftermath of famine. But because of negated reportage we are now belatedly informed of this stupefying tragedy some twenty intolerable years after its original occurrence.

So when the Democratic Youth Party in May of 1992 formally protested the project, 179 members were arrested and their whereabouts kept chronically unknown. Remember, their protest is concerned with a potentially unstable force of "36 billion cubic yards of water." And should faulty construction result in its release, about 400,000 cubic yards of water would come crashing downstream every second. This would engulf in its wake "the populous cities of Shashi, Yichang, Wuhan, and Changsha, imperiling" some "10 million Chinese." Yet the government proceeds within this modernistic cul-de-sac, despite the fact that its technology remains inadequate, "to build the 26 sets of megawatt turbines," along with the electrical generation needed at the heart of the dam. Thus, it is nothing more than a project summoned from the "icon . . . of national prestige." A project led by Qian Zhengying, minister of water resources. This undertaking, much like the rigid testimonials of Mao, is akin to the Great Leap Forward, the heinous arthritics of the Cultural Revolution, and the preventable policy which forged the great floods of Henan. Qian Zhengying, authoress of the latter disaster, seems at present intent on quashing all legitimate dissent, as if she could willfully contain the unforeseen pressures of the unpredictable.

As Audrey Topping points out, "The Yangtze River is actually three rivers in one. Tumbling down from its source in the Tibetan glaciers of the Tangula Mountains," it flows "across the Qinghai-Tibetan Plateau," and "is known as the River to Heaven. From Qinghai it becomes the River of Golden Sands, which flows a thousand miles to Yibin." Its last extension "covering 2000 miles," "is known as the Long River." It cascades through the Three Gorges past Wuhan before spreading its wings through alluvial plains and "winding a path to its mouth in the Shanghai estuary."

Half of China's food is grown along its banks, and it fosters 380 million beings in its wake. Its gorges over millennia have formed a "pantheon of deities," a deluge of "mythical beasts," "passed on by peasants, mandarins, and emperors" like a circular refrain. "The river embodies the mythic image of Old Cathay—the five-clawed celestial dragon symbol of the emperors." It is also the reality of "Lung Wang, the four-clawed dragon king and chief of the water gods . . . reputed to reside in a castle under Goose Tail Rock in Wind Box Gorge." And parallel to Lung Wang exist such species as the Chinese Sturgeon, the finless porpoise, and the native alligator, specific with its indigenous ferocity. But should the dam be built these fauna would be lost forever. Add to this its construction on a fault line, and the scenario of an earthquake transpires, which could trigger its waters and release massive extinction.

The Three Gorges project merely reflects the state endowed brutality of Tiananmen Square. Repression in the name of rote aggrandizement. So this massacre of the infrastructure algebraically equates with the growing arms accrual which the government now pursues with intensity.

Its Su-27 fighter jets imported from Russia, as well as "MIG-31 interceptors, Tu-22 bombers, T-72M main battle tanks, and A-50 airborne warning and control planes" all purchased from its financially ailing neighbor at rock-bottom prices. These acquisitions, part prestigious ornament, but their majority realia, honed for injurious deployment. There are the Paracel and Spratly archipelagoes which China hotly contests against the other countries in the region, the latter being Brunei, Malaysia, the Philippines, Taiwan, and Vietnam. In keeping with this perception of threat China "has built a military airstrip" to accommodate its Su-27 fighters "on Woody Island in the Paracels." Combine this with the Xia, its one nuclear powered ballistic submarine, and its continued nuclear testing at Lop Nur, and you have a government psychically giving way to the negative force of outmoded Western military models. Yes, a despicable quotient of atoms kindled and split in the service of militaristic mirage. As I see it, this Western model for all intents and purposes has become a hovering roundelay of dysfunction.

In keeping with the previous, the Western allurements of Shanghai exist as a replica of a spiritually starved Berlin, and take on the characteristic of the vampiristic craniums of New York and L.A. In a single word, confusion. An invasive ballistic wrath, explosive diacritical poisons, combined with inward dissension as it has evolved since the dictatorial rule of Yuan Shi Kai in 1912, through Chiang Kai-shek and the Kuomintang, running through Mao Tse-Tung and the axial fervor of his peasant-based authority. A series of deleterious mood swings from the warlord Yuan, to the cultural barbarity of the butcher Mao. Leadership in the main has been monolithic, violent, the flesh and blood of the populace has been coerced by hardened formulae, tempered in their aims by blows from theoretical cadres, now the short circuited burst into capital as province.

Lost in these past 80 or so years has been the diverse peculiarity of the countryside, with its ghosts, with its mulberry gusts blowing through impalpable gorges. As if its differences were sealed under a fertile bulletin of grace. Then one can begin to condense the magic of the 67 million who exist outside the majority population of the Han Chinese. I am speaking of the 55 national minorities, among whom are counted the Yi, of the Daliang Shang region, who, until the latter 1950's practiced a "rigid hierarchical slave society." There were actually four levels, the "Black Bones" who were the nobles, then came the "Qunuo or commoners," then the "Ajia, or so called tributary slaves, who lived outside the nobles' households," then at the bottom "the Yaxi, or house slaves, who were forced to live with their noble masters." A negative situation which has ended, yes, but people of a unique stamp normally undetected to the outside onlooker. Within vicinity of the aforementioned Yi lie the cities of Chengdu and Kangding. The former, surrounded by "a golden fringe of rice fields," the latter, "ringed by snow-clad mountains in a valley where the Zheduo River thunders through." Its townspeople "often dump corpses of people into the Zheduo." This is known as "water burial." They also practice another method known as "sky burial"; cutting up the corpse "and feeding the pieces to the vultures." Then cremation or "fire burial," "restricted to the wealthy," and finally "earth burial" preferred by the Han, or those Tibetans greatly influenced by the Han. Conjunctive with the aforesaid was the distressed lama at Hezuo near the Min Shan mountain range who had no skill in calling vultures, so an assistant was hired whose articulations proved fruitful in creating an abundance of birds for the proper eating of the dead. Generally unbearable to the Western mental complex, such practice continues to exist outside of the dominant rhetoric of post-Deng commercial endeavor.

And there exist other acrobatic particulars. The Tu of Qinghai

Province who are related to the Mongols, and who number 160,000. Their girls are constrained to marry by 15, and if an occurrence fails they are symbolically married to heaven. This praxis, called "daitiantou," may account for the numerical poverty of its population. But 600 kilometers beyond the village of Dazhang and the Tu lies "the majestic lamasery of Labrang in southern Gansu Province," with its six colleges of knowledge. These are the "Esoteric . . . Teaching of Buddhism, the Lower and Higher Colleges of Theology, the College of the Wheel of Time, the College of Medicine," as well as "the College of Astronomy." "Completion of all its courses can take as long as 15 years."

Inside the Min Shan mountains another anomaly exists, the Di people. Their written records cease around the year 420 A.D. They have no written language, but are empowered by "a colorful oral history." Their legend has it that "heavens bestowed on humans an abundance of rice covering the entire earth like snow." But a woman mistakenly "stepped on some grains of rice, thereby offending God. God sent the ox to earth to announce His punishment for mankind: Each person was to comb his hair three times a day and eat but one meal a day. By mistake the ox ordered combing of the hair once a day and eating of three meals a day. God was much angered and banished the ox to earth to toil and repent. The ox begged for mercy. First, he claimed he would be ill-treated on earth. God therefore gave the ox horns to defend himself. Second, the ox worried about insect bites. God gave him a tail to drive the insects away. Third, the ox was afraid of being punished if he was to oversleep. So God asked the people to sing to the ox to keep him awake. To this day, the Di always sing whenever they plow their fields with their oxen."

Such concretized mythology totally escapes rational concern, and seeps as a fever from imaginal rootedness.

They occupy the realm of the portentous, the exceptional, the fantastic. And so these Di, these White Horse Tibetans, are kindred with the Miao, in that they radically diverge from the customs of the majority Han. They are a lot of 5 million, over half of whom occupy the zone of Guizhou Province, one of the poorest regions in China. There may be "a hundred distinctive subgroups" with each "speaking a slightly different dialect and maintaining its own traditions and customs." And the Miao "can be divided into five main groups: the Black," the "Red," the "White," the "Blue," and the "Flowery Miao—all desginations based on traditional costume." Both musical and superstitious they are capable of subverting mischief by effectively lying to demons. For instance, "during an offering of food to the demons the Miao might present a piece of pig's leg but call it a whole pig in their prayers. A glass of proffered wine would be inflated to a whole jar or kettle." Such practices extend to the whole of their lives. Before "a marriage could be approved, a chicken had to be killed in front of the parties concerned. After the chicken was cooked whole, the size of both its eyes was examined. If the eyes were identical, it symbolized a happy union. But if they were of different size, it was considered a bad omen and the wedding plans were automatically canceled."

From China, one could create a list of this sort beautiful with anomaly. I could just as easily have mentioned the Muslim Kazaks, or the 70,000 Ge. It is not as it is to the unhoned eye, a monolithic prairie, or a homogenetic trail filled with Communist ingredients. Constrained by limit I can only take down certain sketches as to the power of its human variety. But sadly, I am aware that the Beijing bureaucrats would mechanically annihilate this power, combining its labor within a didactic force field, and would eliminate the camels of the nomads, the "tortilla-like bread" of the Qing, exotically named "sachuisanda." It would eliminate this heterogenesis, and because of this threat there now exists an electric confusion running through this once secretive giant and its enclaves.

On the eastern shore there is the "new uniform" of blue jeans in the "Special Economic Zones" recently created to attract foreign capital and know-how. It is a world of teeming practical mirages. The cities of Amoy, Swatow, Shenzen, and Zhuhai. Zones where the West can mingle Chinese perception with its contradictory staining. "The Continental Grain Company of New York, the East Asiatic Company of Denmark, digital clock radios bearing the J.C. Penney brand." In contradistinction, the oxen still toil within the same motif as an image emblazoned on a tomb 1500 years prior. There is a deadly incoherency at work. Modern energy burns, numerical deadlines are met, yet the countryside still vibrates with mysterious orations to demons. China's five constitutions since 1949 have proved of no working value. Its Campaign for Patriotic Education, largely a failure. Hu Shih, China's greatest scholar in the 20th century has pointed this out. Centralized power in so vast a land mass causes strain in its outer tendons, witness the fractious warlordism at the fall of Yuan's centralized rule. So it can be safely said that this past 80 or 90 years in no way resembles the world that the Romans sought in the beautiful silks of Serica, or the world that the Persians experienced in their acknowledgement of the Chinese mastery of porcelain.

It is a world whose dynasties commenced with the Hsia in 2357 B.C., ending thousands of years later with the fall of the Manchu in 1911. A wayward human geology, full of spectacular consolidations and wagers, so artfully condensed by the author Jean Levi in his novel The Chinese Emperor, concerning the intrigues of the Qin.

The image of China as I stated at the outset, oblique and invehicular. Its size, third in the world with its land mass. An unfathomable border with eleven other countries. A coastline bordering on three seas. Twenty-three provinces and five autonomous border regions. Its "topography . . . often described as . . . forming three levels of elevation, which rise, like steps, from the lowlands on the east coast to the high mountains in the west." And these three elevations are themselves crossed "by east-west trending mountain ranges that subdivide the three elevation regions into nine subregions." Add to this pangolins, and tree shrews, and forest jerboas, and one is then witness to an overwhelming compound.

As for the future and its aftermath, China remains estranged as to reason, as to the motion of its billion plus cohabitants. There is impact to be sure, but to take into account the range of this conflicting Hydra, is to leave one strained, and gasping in a psychic breach, inwardly groping around its unseasonable morass, like the hunger of a Panda, staggering within the meager nutrients of bamboo.

THE EMBLAZONED ONTOGENIC

According to Hegel and Marx, Africa was a land without import, without palpable neural complexity capable of spanning the gulf between history and the teeming protokinetic which spawned it. Until recent account Africa has been rendered as being incapable of planetary fecundation. For instance, the origin of ignescence was attributed to "Peking Man" in Asia, with the Chokontien cave carrying evidential proof of human fire being no earlier than this 500,000 year marker. Yet it has been subsequently shown that fire was originally ignited at Chesowanja, Kenya, 1.4 million years ago by Australopithecus robustus. Or looking further into another misnomer, the Euro-cultural forces have given credit to major artistic culmination at Lascaux without giving proper credit to the carvings achieved at the Apollo cave in Namibia dated at 28,000 B.C., making them "almost twice as old as the Lascaux paintings in the south of France." Going further, there have been confirmations by Richard Leakey of carbon dated carvings going back to 35,000 B.C. in Tanzania, along with paintings found by Frobenius "in the Basuta country of South Africa which dates to the Upper Paleolithic," of "elk in the Khotsa grotto."

Misleading information once championed Ramapithecus "and its close relative Sivapithecus ... as the first hominids," but because of deeper probing it is now seen that Australopithecus was "the earliest true hominid," its important fossil sites having been found at Olduvai Gorge in Tanzania, at Lake Rudolf in Kenya, at Madar in Ethiopia. Then there are the connecting points between Australopithecus and our present stature, these being homo erectus, and homo habilis, followed by the "Broken Hill Man" of Zambia, which has led us to homo sapiens sapiens, "who has the same morphology as modern man." And this is clarified by a "skull found at Laetoli" (in Tanzania) representing "an intermediate specimen between homo erectus and homo sapiens; . . . an archaic sapiens sapiens ... with Grimaldian Negroid features who left Africa about 40,000 years ago to people Europe." The latter's "Aurignacian industry" was already developed when entry into Europe was commenced.

Because the yield from early African humanity is so vivid, the preternatural transit from "prehistory into history" startles by the first flowering of the "Pharaohs of Nubia," who preceded the First Dynasty of Egypt by six or seven generations, and who no doubt were mesmerically immersed in the first human writings found at Uruk and Susa.

CONCRETE

A UBIQUITOUS BUT
VEXATIOUS PRAGMATIC

In the West concrete has taken on the character of the architectonic, the solely pragmatic. It is that which houses restraint, promulgates commerce, so that beings entering and escaping its flanks remain unalterably concerned with its primary status of constant monetary exchange. The latter concern producing an atmosphere of precise but sedentary rancor. A state of mind which functions as barrier, and partakes of an unspoken hostility. Again, a state of mind consumed by massive fixation.

Two words come to mind: cold and anguish. The former partakes "of a temperature much lower than that of the human body," and is also commingled with indifference and death. The latter, the absolute consummation of "great mental or physical pain." What follows are reductive psychic faculties condensed around a core. The human continuum is then lowered to a hypostatic level condoned by a grammar based upon intuitive debility.

We come to the genesis of the modern construct with the advent of the Englishman Joseph Aspdin, who in 1824 patented his invention of Portland cement. It is a process achieved by the bonding of "fine and coarse aggregate particles with cement paste, which is a mixture of cement and water." Its physical base is calcareous, "such as limestone or chalk, and from alumina- and silica-bearing material, such as clay or shale." The raw materials are ground, then heated in a rotary kiln at about 2500 degrees Fahrenheit. Then the material "sinters and partially fuses into balls known as clinker," which are "cooled and ground to a fine powder, with Gypsum . . . added to control the speed of setting when cement is mixed with water." Because its tensile strength is low, "steel reinforcement is placed where it is necessary for structural members to resist tensile forces."

From this remove, we come to "skeleton construction" in the Chicago of the 1880's. "Built floor by floor, steel-frame structures can be erected to great heights." "The first steel-framework skyscraper was built within its confines in 1884," the Home Insurance Building designed by engineer-architect William LeBaron Jenny. This was followed by the Rand McNally Building in 1890, and the Masonic Temple in 1891, which paved the way for New York's neo-Gothic Woolworth Building constructed in 1914, thereby giving rise to the Empire State which was built in 1931. Now we live with the Sears Tower, and the John Hancock Center, imposing on the atmosphere monolithic verticality.

This is a pattern which has been reinvented in other teeming enclaves such as Tokyo, Toronto, and Los Angeles. And in none of these bastions has the commercial ideal thought to question itself, thought to give itself any other approach than as a specter of dominance, as a monstrous emblematic of capital epitomized by a wrenching and overwhelming hypnotic. These are zones where even the material sun is occluded, where ruinous and inevitable squabblings transpire, where the wreckage of emotional persons is the outcome of the daily profit margin. So for me, the alarming repetition of the metropolis is nothing more than the studied face of an economically rapacious evil, ostentatious and replete with darkened subliminal motives. Its gift to the world being psycho-physical realias which remain hostile and aloof to the spontaneous magic of the moment.

In contrast, attempts have been made to form more acceptable habitations for expressing the human spirit. I'm thinking of Le Corbusier's Unité d'Habitation in Marseilles, and "the several structures he designed . . . at Ahmedabad, in India." Or the work of the Brazilian Lúcio Costa, who "endeavored to make modern architecture regionalistic in intent and to adapt it to tropical environments." Which brings me to the Dymaxion House, and the Geodesic Dome of Buckminster Fuller. His advocacy of using "ever-decreasing amounts of materials," his commitment to limitless human geographical mobility, are hallmarks of an energy far removed from the static foundries of objective suffocation, which say, spellbind the citizens of Manhattan as they take their frenzied constitutionals from one interior aversion to another. The human being cast about within an uneasy yet propulsive monologue, who suffers within a private necrotic drama, enacted on the stage of a cold and embittered theater. As Paolo Soleri points out, architectures which void the breathing of the planet cannot suffice as lodging which inspires the scope of the human species. They can inspire a continuous weaving of villainy, of mistrust, of perpetually kindled frustration. So the population remains haunted, burdened with limited symmetry, spewing recalcitrant vapors like fumes from old sesterces. So I think of movement in this mode as plagued with sinister disfigurement.

In this singular light that I've cracked, the city planner exists as symbolic of the stamina of repression. Of course the linear immobility that results from this or that plan, the static intentional measurement that corrodes all fate, that blocks the modus of self-engenderment. He or she settles on the day-to-day linguistics of profit, with no other measure secured for the consciousness. Therefore the modern businessperson always seeking the sullen quaternary walls, the blazeless rote of a ceiling. Held in like cattle, they function by accretion of mass. Yet they exist only as figments in Marx's brilliantly argued surplus value. They are fused with self-deprecating priority always maliciously resolved to turn on their equals. Again buildings are designed to enhance this embitterment.

I look at postmodern landmarks much in the way Breton subversively described the landmark in *Nadja*. Discussing the latter, Renée Hubert points out that "the statues of Etienne Dolet and Henri Becq do not function as stone portraits asserting an identity, but as strange, almost absurd, sources . . . These cumbersome, ornate masses of stone paradoxically undermine our sense of stability and thrust us onto a road where attraction or repulsion acts as a stimulant making us aware of the absurdity of solid, recognizable landmarks."[1]

AT THE DEPTH OF
THE RADIOLARIANS

As Radiolarians, they solely exist in the "Pelagic," in seething micro-hemispheres, implying at all instants the three principal depths of the sea, the euphotic, the dysphotic, and the aphotic.

In the euphotic zone there exists ubiquitous transparency, herbivorous imbibing, and in its "Neritic Province" close to the shore, exist rays and sharks, pteropods, and squids. While still in the "Neritic," and just below the euphotic, one comes to the most difficult subdivision of the sea. It is the "Neritic-Benthic or Littoral Zone," where "water movement" is "bounded by the high- and low-water marks of the highest spring tides and which varies in extent with the geographical location, and a sublittoral or nontidal zone, which extends from low-water to the edge of the continental shelf." What next transpires is the division of the "Eulittoral or Tidal Subzone" where weather exists "as we know it on land." Below the "Neritic-Benthic," it remains the harshest zone because of its scarcity of sustenance, because of its "buffeting of waves," where its levels of life must be of utmost resistance, like "rockweed," or "barnacles," or "sand bugs." Yet after such turbulence, another demarcation persists, which is the "Subtidal Subzone," with its octopi, its urchins, and its "prochordates such as Amphioxus." Saying such, we have descended from the radiance of the euphotic, yet have not left the lateral realia of the "Neritic," where conversely, one can find the ancient Squirrel fish at the upper "Littoral" level voraciously "active at dusk."

When we range beyond the "continental shelf " into the "Oceanic Province" the dysphotic appears. In this dimly lit zone herbivores are absent, and bioluminescence begins to unfold. I am thinking of the "Phylum Ctenophora," with its "Mnemiopsis," its "Pleurobranchia," the former possessing luminescence, but both species being "exclusively pelagic," and capable of existing in all "seas of the world." But what more solely specifies the fauna at this depth is its "diurnal migration moving up toward the surface at night and returning to the depths during the day." The fish at these extents are of the genus "Dolichopteryx," which can grow to lengths of 4 inches, "have tubular eyes," and like the "Omosudius lowei" are at home at this level of visual equivocation.

Going deeper, into the apparitional realm of the aphotic, the "sea devil" is found at 3,000 meters. And because of the obfuscation at this remove, the female is endowed "with a luminous lure on her nose that she vibrates to attract prey." Through instinctive relation her male companion laterally attaches himself to her body at maturity, and becomes nothing more than a necessitous "source of sperm." One of the more interesting facts concerning this realm is the coexistent lack of "swimming speed," coupled with a vicious characteristic as exampled by the "predacious Atlantic viperfish."

Admittedly, what's been related so far has been a compressed biotic of the sea, with its five zones of heat, ranging from the "Arctic" and the "Boreal," to the "Tropic." Of course the factor of heat is of uttermost essence in that the sea is seen to live at various gradations of respiration, as exemplified by its lesser and greater vehicular thermals found in its movements off lands from Labrador and Newfoundland, to Cape Hatteras and the Bahamas. These differences exist, and are coalescent with the magnitude which subsists throughout the "forty million square miles" of water which envelops the "ocean floor" of the planet.

So, with such specifics in mind, I've finally come to the "Flagellates" who form the "greatest ... linking groups in evolution." Some carry "chlorophyll" and are "photosynthetic," while others "eat food such as decayed substances as do animals." They are most important in converting "light to Carbohydrates." The "Flagellates," being derived from the protozoans, are partially represented by the "Crytomonads," the "Noctiluca," and the "Radiolarians." And these latter, earlier mentioned, are optically exquisite because of their "siliceous skeletons," which tend to hypnotize the eye as would a glinting mirage of glass. They generate motion by means of their inscrutable "pseudopodia," by means of droplets of oil in "the body." And what is most striking, at the more difficult fathoms, the radiolarians seem infinite. This occurs, when they flow into the depths like cascades. Because at death they permeate their habitat with the "radiolarian oozes" of their silicate skeletal remains. Unlike the soluble "calcareous skeletons of foraminiferans," their osteology is insoluble and is resistant to entropy, thereby forming as vitreal phantoms near the ocean bottoms, an image available only to the observer concerned with the magic of "Pelagic" poetics.

A HUMAN INTENSITY

MONOGRAPHS, MEMORIALS, MEETINGS

CHARLES FOURIER

SPARK OF THE HARMONIAN LIGHTNING WHEEL

The next revolutionary wave, if it is to achieve sufficient
power and breadth, must be a synthesis of all previous ideas,
and must unite, into one cohering mass, all the "ghosts."
—KENNETH WHITE ON CHARLES FOURIER

Like a phantom under the smoke of a splintered kerosene chrysalis, there is the image of Charles Fourier weaving his trenchant solstice needles from a spiral of sonorous vapor and jade. And with a jagged marmoset lisping by his side, and a penetrant crystalline stylus spinning in his fingers, he emits the power to calculate beautific bodily fields and heresy. And by bodily fields I mean the openness, the perfect right and honor of pleasure, and by heresy, I mean the seasoning of his journey with alchemical hissing and turbulence against civil fraud and disorder.

So it is that Fourier seizes us with fire and the ecstasy of dreaming. The bird with its flaming thermal escape into a powerful uranian clair-audience, alive with syncopation and stillness. The utopian endeavor condensed in this image inspired by the writer with the hand of thirst, who opened 19th century thought to "Phalanxes," who cast passion into a higher realm of scarlet, into another register of vibration, wholly above the principles of shattering and panic. Here one found the fire restored to a pelican's rested armor, a shellfish resurrected by internal summas of greenness. He superseded reason, and merged the separations through "variety and . . . change," and created in the process an anti-transfixture, thereby transmuting psychic arthritics by the a priori action of God, spawned in the fire of the senses.

If given a utopian radical optics, one could magically trace the movements of diphthong gazelles, or place in the beam of one's brilliance a destiny of dreaming cobra striped zebra. The aforementioned, quite in keeping with Fourier's ramblings conducted at an inward pitch, with the power to pursue its own powers at the level of an invisible and self-sustaining orbit. A mind Breton described with "a pre-eminent gift for reason and a taste for vaticination." A mind, unlike the timing of the nunnery, that was able to envision "swing-carts . . . in the castle of cherry gardeners" by means of a ferocious imaginal breathing. A world, a Harmonian blend, where each specific action remained unconstrained to duty; where isolation was broken down and the combined effects of the passions merged into an overgathering of momentum, a supremely positive momentum. To him, no moral surgery was applicable, no philanthropic apogee was embodied, cooling the heat of life with a topical monument of reason. Labor for him was an act of pleasure, an act of nobility, a poem of fantastic enticement. An atmosphere without envy, or jealousy, or acts of repressive sublimation. The collective was the power with its marvelous abolition of regressive motor resistance, thereby engendering the primal elixir within the cerulean terrain of the vivifying portion.

As a young clerk at Marseilles he is transmogrified by the pitching of rice into the sea. He forever turns against the rancid speculation, and the commercial psychosis which spawned it. It was decisive; the individual need no longer live at the behest of contrived abysses, tainted by aggressive structural stagnation. For him, the wind began to live again with the force of aboriginal burning, and the Sun was colored green by the free "astronomers of Asia."

So, from this unobstructed nerve arose attractional passion, no longer subject to the blinding stains of the social order. The latter always seeking devices of grit and disorder, where blood was extracted by rapacious plesiosaur's mechanics. A vile, unending impasse, stained by abbreviated fuels of misfortune. A system of profit which corroded renewal. For Fourier, the antidote was the lifting of water from minerals so as to test the true variety of the spectrum. The beauty of nopal, or an aerial herd of eagles, became part of a sensuous, unceasing inventiveness. In contradistinction, there was the civilized moat where arson was waged against the throat and the skin, so that the body was held hostage within the blackened methodology of the furnace. A starkness inscribed by linear invariety, by a smoke-filled psyche without rubies or lightning. The body rotted, the soul wavered, the spirit was excluded. So therefore the pedestal of regularity formed a desultory pinnacle of stability. The worker was constantly rewarded for the same arthritic facility, the unending work day, the revolving discussion and interchange of matter. But for Fourier there was no longer the projected pheromone of hostility, the mental pillage of the blindfolded task. He annulled the hordes of fiscal armies producing unripened fragments for dictatorial consumption. And he knew the constant blood ache, and the seal of repression.

Society was no more than a snake, slipping across one's shoulders, leaving shallow wounds of poison, which allowed one to live, which refused to one's body the simple comfort of death. So there was living for the daily wage, the constant exposure to supreme axial barbarity.

He was witness to this miserable zenith, with its macro confusion of empire announcing a call to arms with a flaccid and disintegrating bugle. A bugle which Fourier saw as a call which arrested, which stunted, which institutionally inverted. And it was no more to him than "the latest of our scientific chimeras." A crab conducting sound with a meandering and parasitical rhapsodics. He proceeded to depict from this alarm the parasitic nature in bold poetic relief. First, the incoherent family unit with its activity of tedious trauma, brought on by the fact of industrial division, which simultaneously proceeded from the separated household. A life innately feeble, like a pictographic mud leash, without the variety and flair of an interactive tension. Then there were the sadistic codifications of the "ARMIES," and the "MERCHANTS," and the "spies," all reduced to a practical insignificance, in that they remained idle when not productive in their respective negativities. He scrutinized the "agents of transportation" who, he reported, through "their ignorance and improvidence increase the number of shipwrecks tenfold." Of course, the plummeted quality of the "MANUFACTURES" was disturbing, they who engaged the power of a duplicitous and hypothetical excellence, supported by a dire but ubiquitous juridical folly.

Fourier contended that the power of attractive labor would supersede the necessity of such crime as it existed at the core of parasitical dysfunction. He compiled data on top of data concerning the resistives of these dysfunctional wolverines, empowered within the scope of drudgery and want. What followed was his central insight concerning the lack of living desire, the condensed and unarguable brutality, which created an inevitable abstention from labor. "If the master is out of sight" he observed, "the laborers stop; if they see a man or cat pass all are in a stir, masters and servants leaning upon their spades ... gazing in order to divert themselves."

Life in this context was no more than an exhaustive famine, an exercise for imbibing venom. Yes, it was a testament to unerring disfigurement, to a task of searing taboos and consignments. Fourier himself bemoaned his designation as "commercial traveler," like an ironical fish conjoined to bony sand diluents. Nevertheless, he engaged the air of liberation, condemning the economics of his life span as limited to the "analysis of existing evil." By its tacit passivity, he saw that this discipline empowered extortion, made do with depravity. He roundly condemned its abstract optical glances concerning the Irish hunger of 1826. And its natural lack of antidote he abhorred. The apologists of his era like Dugald Stewart, or M. J. B. Say, he classified as authors of sophistry, and extollers of anguish. Hunger for the authorities was nothing but a cunning technical drama, where one could sort out and contain the controlling points. And here we get to his fundamental dissidence against middle men; their extorting, their sowing of disorder at the core of exchange. The producer and the consumer blunted, kept apart and placed on a permanent footing of rivalry. The general good was never the goal. And Fourier brilliantly chronicled this generic malevolence, when the physician was seen as wishing his fellow citizens "genuine cases of fever," the architect psychologically courting multiple conflagrations, with the courts of justice skillfully vitalized by crime. Nothing more than legalized disruptions, contrived pecuniary motifs, based upon a model of obligatory dishonor. In contrast, within Fourier's Harmonian world, axial monotony was broken and transmuted by the inward rotation of pleasure. And for Fourier, this pleasure was an a priori given, an instinctual testament, untainted by mirages. For him it expressed our original unity as living beings, our primeval dispensation from the power on high. The restraint, the peculiarity of segregation, is only a rational and subsequent contrivance. Therefore he knew that the civil life was maimed by a lack of variety, by a lack of surreptitious flow and inspiration. The social body suffers with nothing but bread, with the delights of the body and the palate condemned. Analogy is reduced to doubt, and copulation commences in a furnace of snares.

In his world of Harmonian ardor, he knew the sparks of attraction would electrically adhere to an honor. And that honor was variety, so fruitfully exemplified by the butterfly flitting across a splendiferous array of nectars. Labor will last for no more than two hours, with verbal exchange across all regions of difference. The upper and the lower, the lighter and the darker, brought into harmonious confluence. From the cradle throughout life monotony was excluded, replaced by the nuance and refinement of consumption.

The result was a utopian colored being, a spectrum colored being, drinking from a chalice of indigo and saffron. A gorgeous roundelay of balance where the being was infused with the savvy of intrigue. The subtext inspired by a contradictory spikenard. As if the whole collective were invested by a magnified divination, able to meander, and asymmetrically collect jade from a dune, and build from their findings a palace, capable of changing its visual and aural congruence, through the different shadings in the moments of the day. The cherry pickers, the lovers, the gardeners, the abstractionists, entering and re-entering the magic of its confines, all of one action, playing with the fire of a priori being.

And Fourier, who struck the first pure seed of utopia, imbibed the pri-mal ray, the aboriginal utterance, and transmitted its spark, which turned the lightning wheel, the Harmonian lightning wheel, with its riveting assessment, with its circular attainment of openness and feeding.

ON CLAYTON ESHLEMAN

I met him at an activists' event. An event concerned with ridding the death czars and contras from Reagan's El Salvador. Or was it an event proto to Reagan protesting a tension which was culminate in the Contras. In hindsight, it was an auspicious demarcation for me. We talked, he invited me to his abode, work was exchanged, mutual insights were broached. Upon seeing a small sample of my writing he suggested publication. He encouraged me to use his name as a password. River Styx in St. Louis accepted my missive. It was my first poem published. "Mountainslope Swimming in Detroit" emerged from the shadows. Then "Australian X-Ray Painting" was included in the second issue of *Sulfur*, his magazine. I have never looked back.

In his initial generosity I glimpsed his fervor, his turbulent dedication on behalf of poetry as a penetrant alchemic. For him the voice burns like a sun, reddish and brooding, appearing at tellurian twilight. And it is this sun in him which has brought to English the great "cecropias" of Césaire, the skittish sea quakes of Vallejo. Add to this his own exploratory shifts, always repealing and going forward, converting into poetry his own endemic dangers.

For me, it has been comradeship fused by poetic commitment, punctuated by silence and warm regard.

It has been a contact seminal with endurance which has led to meetings and friendships with other penetrant practitioners of the written art, among them Anthony Seidman and James Heller Levinson.

Knowing Clayton Eshleman is to know one has practices in confronting the source of psychic fissure, of one who has given his whole soul and body to the explorational depths rooted in the vertigo of poetic kinematics.

THE IMPACT OF A LIVING BEING

AUSTIN BLACK / 1928–1993

How many beings do we know that actually qualify as living? And by living not limiting the word to the circulatory force of blood in the body, or to an ironic statistical verve, but impact in terms of the higher existence, the higher character whose legacy transcends quotidian forgetfulness with the pristine qualities of nerve. The ability to challenge, to thrive from the heavenly wheat of contradiction.

For me, this higher persona is a being who casts spells, but not in the popular sense, or through the accessible ray of a pejorative atomics. So when I think of a genuine being, of a being who dueled, and at moments superceded the dialectic, I think of Austin Black, (Ishmael as we called him) charging up stellar ramparts with his living alchemical blade. He would say, here is the road, here is the blinded lightning path. He would say, I have wounded the dragons and they want to discuss my access to pleromas. He was relentless, with his mind of wizardry and penetration. He explored the many homes of the absonant, and the spires of treachery marked by diamond and wisdom, and the momentary seasonings flecked with disaster.

Yes, he had the impact of a mesmerizing wiseness. And as a young poet in the throes of linguistic thirst, I would sit on anonymous afternoons collecting the scent of his conjury and possession. I was not looking for biographic methodologies, or one to one applicability as to circumstance and dates, but nutrients for the upper mind, for the superior skill of balance. From his motionless sonorities I absorbed weights of sun and rain, poetically growing into my wingspan, taking longer and longer flights from the cliff. With our mutual ally Jim Henderson, discussion transpired within

the context of names like René Guénon, Hazrat Inayat Khan, George Ivanovitch Gurdjeff, Sri Aurobindo, revolving in a discourse of grand and medicinal insight. And there was always an invisible subtext to this discourse, an a-secular lightning sussurating spells by implied kinetic. For he knew that higher contemplation is invisible, that it ceases to connote a measurable quantity. It is the weightless self which explores the vertical mystery. Therefore I gathered insights from this circle which gave me the authority of a fabulous trespasser's law. And I mean the law of mental mesmerics capable of uprooting scorpions from stone.

When commencing biography there is always the danger of the horizontal view, its moral limitations, its snares enclosed in habituation and sentiment. Ishmael never existed in the operatives of such hesitations. There was always his courage against the truculence of opposition. Whether exposing corruption in the East St. Louis financial chambers, or "on the San Bernardino . . . Court House steps" fasting six days and six nights with loaded pistol in hand. For Ishmael it was always the symbolic dying in order to raise new life for the living. So here was a man engaged in cyclical combat against imprisoning matter. I say cyclical because his mind had left the linear staging grounds and had taken on a circular grace where his enemies could only stammer at the coming and going of a ghost. A man with an inner magnet who pledged his cause as risen above the vanity of lower theatrics. To poetically construe him, one would have to sense the inward motion of a planet, hearing its symphonic blueness, its singular madrigal army at star rise. You would see his psychic wingspread soar above the entropy of the culture, you would see him cancel rancid deliriums with a glance, with a charged gesture of pointing. In order for him to strike initial sparks, he knew it was his right, and his right alone to send explosive signals, converting pressure and diamonds from the surrounding social chaos.

Here I do not seek to scale his integrations with a rumination on dates, but to seek the source of his iconic intent as he existed amongst us as a human intensity. Essentially his was a quest to break down monuments, to unchain fetters. To commence upon such a quest, he had washed from himself the infirmity of labels, cleared himself of the haunted inner cripplings, so that he was able to exist within a procession of clarity. So when such incisiveness exists, when the esoteric pulses under force of such necessity, quite naturally it encounters exoteric impediment, which engenders a chronic misperception. Misperception from the exoteric point of view tends to drown out and capitulate all meanings to the force of its view. Thus Ishmael was held to a standard which he had long since surmounted. A state of mind which sought to cancel him, which sought a flameless hieratics and darting. Because as one rises into the less tangible callings, one is confronted by a stunning, but lifeless propaganda. Stunning in the sense of its backwardness, the exhaustive nature of its crudity. It exists without current, without the subtle proof of its barbaric engenderment. And there is always the implication that nothing can be accomplished without material labor, that the results of one's life journey should bear tangible, commonly seasoned fruit. Therefore the fruit most actively accounted for is superficially colored by conspicuous accoutrement, or a fleeting popular fame, both incapable of threatening the common person's daily nausea of work in the service of the national deficit.

Having broken the hold of this despicable verbatim, Ishmael was a radical, a spirit of contained moral lightning. Because of his insight he understood the fundamental cruelty of the colonial mentality as it reacts to its powers in places as removed as Belfast and Watts. He who lived by interior resistance, he who fasted on water and sky, he who confronted the political frailty of the status quo. So every dawn he took his stave to the vampire's heart, and declaimed his principles in the language of rotation.

In his out of print book, *Tornado In My Mouth*, he proclaims the power to copulate on lightning bolts, meeting a "Patagonian" whom he joins "flying with locust armies . . . ," putting "a dot at the end of the Warsaw Treaty, in feverish straining excitement."

Lines emblazoned like traceries of phosphorous, which leap like squirming fish from cosmic stellar iridium. Lines as rare as a Malay eagle wafting through the canopies with an inclement rigor. He had the movement of a master in exile, and only would he pause to investigate his motion, to take in the tomes that inspired him. His quest in essence was for an old integral balance, old in the sense of its Egyptian, and pre-Egyptian motifs. Balance implying, centering at the core of fecundity, floating in synthetic complexity. Having returned to the powerful pre-existence of Greece, he found a realia as precise as the constant mathematics of wheat, where the stars were first counted and "named." "Thus the Ethiopian of Thebes named stars of inundation . . . Aquarius, those stars under which the Nile began to overflow; stars of the ox or bull, those under which they began to plow; stars of the lion, those under which that animal, driven from the desert by thirst, appeared on the banks of the Nile; stars of the sheaf, or of the harvest virgin, those of the reaping season; stars of the lamb, stars of the two kids, those under which these precious animals were brought forth . . ."

Here was a man working within a heritage at least 17,000 years distant. I'm speaking of the origin of the zodiac at 15,000 B.C.; and it is at this origin from which Ishmael worked, from the first tribes of Egypt. He did not ascribe to the psychic incarceration of the African diaspora. He set a vehement tone which was simultaneous with a working Nubian methodology. Therefore he always spoke with a jolt of libelous rubies. Libelous in the sense that his very electrical current had nothing but venom for the inverted scale of post-Grecian propaganda which hails the Saxon as the higher human principle. Because there is always this subtle presentiment in the daily life we are forced to lead, which assigns the invirtuous characteristic to the nonwhite genetic, as though the African were fed from the origins of life by neurosis. As though the visage which ice assumes took flight from a superior model, and came screaming form God via the northern viaducts of constriction. And from this Northern model came the prejudice that darker races were electrically salacious, and emerged in this life with a connubial imprint from demons. Darkness being synonymous with occipital damnation, melanin being a curse spun from infelicitous reptilian fire. Breaking the mental hold of the Christos, or peering into the heavens over and above that abusive scope of the gendarme, Ishmael understood that Sumer and Chaldea were connected to the original conundrum of living. That the stars, like enriched auroral stones, were capable of projecting his mind into a zone of incessant illuminal wattage. Thus he ascribed to the first proto-sun, to the fabulous fumes of the first proto-rains.

As Ishmael would attest, the Black warrior male is constantly tested by brushes with extinction. The lynchings, the insidious mental sniping, by ex-enslavers, by murderers who equate the Southern integument with the accursed meat of spiders. And by southern integument, I mean Morocco and Timbuktu, and the people who draw the vevers in Haiti. He knew the threat of death quickens the life force, bringing one's courage to a brightened alchemical pitch, allowing sight, across an expanded human field, like an x-ray with venom, seeing the disaster of our present living dimension in the Euromaterial rapaciousness of thought. A disease which had no power to shake him, which had lost all grip on his soul. His power evolved from "the famous city of Susa," rather than the lynching stables of Alabama, from the early "diorite of Magan," rather than the brutal sweating in dark plantation fields. In consequence, he lost the slaves' interior stealth, the deprecated monitor's imbalance, ceasing to see himself in sunken secondary shafts, spoiled from self-invasions of terror. A man who had lifted the thorns from his brain, a man who had exploded the spies in his heart. Therefore, in the midst of the in-illuminables he was the nettling green flame who spoke with wondrous Dravidian authority. He who challenged prostrated totems, he who took the deluded Christian to task for an engrained tellurian duplicity. As to ubiquitous distraction he was immune. As to the knavery and minor stratagems of culpable Black apologists, he remained steadfastly undaunted. And I mean by the latter, those members of the diaspora living in strict defense of their servitude. Those members, who've forgotten their brands, and the "red pepper rubbed into their lacerated flesh." Unlike these members he remained fanatically incoerced by appeals to appeasement. He never forgot the collective scar upon the soul of those whose natural orientation claimed kinship with mystery. He saw America as the home of the auction block where our ancestors suffered, priced in tandem with hogs and various objects and crops. Thus, his intensity, was not mere mercurial embroilment, nor a spate of undeveloped aggression. He displayed the bearing of the runaway, of the opalescent maroon, instinctive with dignity throughout collision and brimstone. For he knew an active clairaudience was culled from mesmeric poppies of dissonance.

As he stated in his 1972 lecture, "Art Forms Beyond Mentation," for the artist who raises his "vibration" the result is "dissonance," "always the feeling of aloneness and sorrow." He stated further that "The artist must always act as pioneer . . . he can never be ordinary," never be the refugee of palatial accommodation perched upon the notion of antivivification. For Ishmael there was always kinship with the intramercurial, with wild explosional purity, with the dual conspiracy of "exposure" and "initiation." For him, there was only the accent of a living verbal honor, the ethics of a flaming astral good. So here is the circuitous biography of a man who was able to hunt down fiends and secure their abdication. And by fiends I mean those regressive powers, those deadly conservationists concerned with securing and freezing racist social mores. Therefore his energies were focused at extreme height and extreme depth, and he became incapable of the arrogant lisp, or of conducting his power like a dualistic king gone mad within him chambers of confinement. No, his primary act was to raise one's forces above the secondary powers of the mind. To raise in a listener's being the fastidious conundrum within the rising of a blue uncertain dimension.

A life of habit, an exercise in banditry? Hardly. I can truly say that here was a man committed to a plane above conditioned social terror, climbing a blank horizon tree, honed by prolific turpentines of Asia, by the ubiquitous solar spirals of Egypt, burning in his mane like cosmic he-goats and lions. Until the end he remained the exhaustive ascensional leper, the man from the Sun holding his heretical dowsing rod, as if traveling across the sea like an old Ethiopian arriving at Palenque. Therefore he saw the Christos as a fabricated destiny, as a false equational talisman formed from "pagan messiahs." "Osiris and Horus of Egypt, Krishna of India, Mithra of Persia . . . Adonis of Babylonia . . ." "There are born of a virgin . . . their births are heralded by a star; they are born . . . in a cave or stable; they are slain . . . by crucifixion; they descend into hell, and rise from the dead at the beginning of spring . . ."

The original Gods were Black, and were the original hypnotic redeemers. This he knew with a fervor. And it is in this vibrational key that he studied the old Biblical king Melchizedek. A study conducted at the end of his days, not from Euro-Christian acquiescence, but Melchizedek as higher persona of light. Throughout his investigation there was no need to wrangle over the ragged dispensation of a shattered European psyche.

Therefore he asks, what is the realia of the planetary afterlife? What is the dominant foliage of the body and its flight throughout the dark invisible realms?

Thus his defiance took him beyond the borders of waking, beyond the mental eclampsias, beyond the programmed psychic rot. And it is from this level that he saw the negative amplification implied in the role of Black churches. Their old colonial role of tempestuous passivity in which a stagnant inner form is transformed once a week into a habitual catharsis, viewed in most cases by a cold Nordic savior staring down on the ritual with a malignant indifference. Yes, the image of a savior with an eye like a young English governor in the Congo. Therefore, the interior African summa missing, not in its outward upheaval, but in its inner clinchings, in its restrictive metaphysical constant. Because the singing transpires in the shadows of judgment ruled by a fickle and malicious father, whose learnings rest with the brutality of a cosmic governing opaqueness. Like Damas, he embodied the runaway, the maroon, the blasphemous eagle who soars to the heights. And it was Ishmael who helped confirm this spirit in me, which I've practiced since the age of later adolescence. It was he who helped me cross the sweltering mental dunes with an electric kind of honor, with a perilous kind of grace.

Having passed from this life, he continues to haunt the upper condition with a lyrical mesmerics, as a fiery incanonical wizard. Although he has slipped through the sun-door, his image has refused to vanish from my lips.

ACKNOWLEDGMENT

WILL ALEXANDER / 1912–1998

The tone of his generation one of defeated archery, of success gone awry, of destiny insidiously stung by a swift moving poison. My father, one of the victims of this era, victims of an ingallant democracy, never allowed to form their proper foci, or hone their inborn skills within the scope of American camaraderie. Instead, the lynch rope, and its galling dialectic of psychic servitude.

I am speaking of the emerging Black male and his maturation between the years of the middle 1930's and the latter part of the 1950's. A beleaguered brethren, whose peak energy was sapped away by hand to hand combat with apartheid. This odyssey was fruitfully punctuated by the universal interjection of the Second World War. I say fruitfully because domestic apartheid was forcefully cracked, allowing the Black male a facile movement through its interstice, due to the general challenge of war. Hitler had proclaimed his 1,000 year Reich encoded with assorted venoms, and there was Imperial Japan, and the theatrical skull of Mussolini. So all hands became bound to the cause. But even as collective effort transpired there remained insidious racial ranking, my father for instance being allowed to rise no higher than Chief Steward in the Jim Crow Navy.

I must stress here that this writing in no way concurs with nepotistic outbreak, nor is it corrosively singed by sentimental flashback. No, I am simply speaking of a man, Will Alexander, who carried a nascent, triplicate propensity, for writing, mathematics, and French; and who was able to carry on correspondence in a flexible vehicular French. And if allowed to develop in this register, I think of Yves Bonnefoy, who was permitted sustained praxis in these exact propensities, writing, mathematics, and the love of a foreign language.

A man of insight and focus who, in a less savage circumstance would have been leading the way for me as poet/painter, rather than waiting for this belated assessment of his powers. And one must remember that during the peak of his energy there occurred 4 to 5 lynchings a day in places such as Texas, Mississippi, and his native Louisiana. Being a genuine survivor of the Red Flag era, he was conversant with the practice of the NAACP, flying a red memorial flag from the windows of its Harlem office every time reported lynchings occurred. And it is on record that study of this atmosphere took on more than a passing interest for the Nazis in sculpting their maniacal roulette of Aryan superiority. Their trenchant observation of the day to day workings of the American South, with its accoutrements of torture, its insidious surveillance, its physical assault, paralleled their operational maturity during this very time, until the fall of the Reich in May, 1945.

Unswayed by this policy of domestic brutalization, my father carried on the independent spirit of family land ownership, which dated back to the obscure year of 1897. You see, when no hurricane of doubt transfixes the psyche, an incorrigible plenitude seems to existentially transmute the seeming losses one incurs into strength. His early writings lost, his attempts at scholarship maliciously circumvented, his membership in unions curtailed due to no other factor than his color. Nevertheless, over time he rose above these unalterable dissensions, remaining a penetrant student of life.

At the present remove, he remains a symbol of a collective racial fate as it occurred during the time of the Second Great War. An incriminating reminder of the continuing racial schism which infernally illumines official American pronouncement, as it continues to deny its dominant hand in this ongoing culpability.

NATHANIEL MACKEY

''AN ASHEN FINESSE''

His writing, a vivid singularity, an incursion, sidelong, metamorphic with philosophical incision. It is language as susurrant usage, as hypnotic sonar, incantatory, as it connects the abyss of the mind to its empyreal upper extremes. Which simultaneously allow his passages to hover, dart, rebel, poised as they are by inward prestidigitation as balance.

Again, a lyrical index of sonar, like permutations gathered from radial eclipse patterns. Replete in the fiction and the poetry is the spin and counter-spin, much in common with "the vibratory field" of Mayan numerical identity. There emerges from his compost of themes, an electrical summa, unlimited in its ability to soar and disrupt itself, and just as quickly momentarily condense itself to form angles that astonish. For instance, in the first few pages of *Bedouin Hornbook*, he crosses Egypt and Haiti with the voice of Ogotemmeli. Make no mistake, whenever one has contact with the writing of Nathaniel Mackey one is immediately ensnared by its sense of vatic weaving. As he says in his poem, "Dogon Eclipse," "I see no boats but hear the waters break." Thus, reading his work is like picking up odors, and transposing scents, like oneiric contradiction and blending.

Not a dubious refraction, but an incendiary sensation which obliterates division between the waking life and the tree of dreaming. And this sensation exists as a simultaneous canal between the poetic works and the fiction, combined by language which empowers them like waters which kindle. An occulted flair if you will, fueled in the sapience of infected calligraphy. And by infected, I mean a nomadic calligraphy, wandering, spinning off dark incalculable rhythms, its overtones humming like a compost of entanglement.

Both his poetry and his fiction partake of a level existing outside the stable zodiac of definitives. I mean, the stabilized invicta, the compartmentally rendered. Much the way a Bedouin's movements correspond with the waves of the sands. In this sense, Nate Mackey coheres as a pilgrim of the uncharted, who stutters throughout the mantic, skittish, unassembled spinning. It seems he has absorbed a basic chronicle of hearing indigenous to that level of mind unaffected by Western mental bifurcation. And this realia of bifurcation is nothing more than a harvest of restriction, which concludes that Europe and the northern lands of the Americas possess the culminate criteria by which the accredited must exist. This is a condition which Wilson Harris addresses as the "block function," which sanctions a reality which excludes unprecedented thoughts and peoples, and utopian splendor of language. Now to draw character upon such exclusivist's rapport is not something you will find in any of Mr. Mackey's fiction. It is not character focused by monolithic sculpting, but character as fluidic awareness. Lambert, Drenette, Penguin, Aunt Nancy, function simultaneously as distinct, but collective presences, like a whole magnetically aligned with its parts. And I do not mean alignment in a linear sense, but in the manner in which prestidigitation harmonizes by means of angular, unexpected impact. Lambert, Drenette, Penguin, and Aunt Nancy exist as magical rivulets of insinuation. Not in the manner of dramatic dénouement, or accessible fictive, but as essentials of permutation. These characters respirate for me, like the magic aftermath of an unsullied breathing. Not as labored creations from a preplanned littérateur, but characters who take on the presence of an interior vivacity.

Having said such, one never feels committed to the limits of a character's axial limitations, to a life which accrues within the depth of static acreage. On the contrary, there are shifts, erosions, fractals, loopings. Therefore, each of his dated entries exists as a tool, as a necessity which sculpts the improvisational dust, like "a curious borderline stance between the compelling and the merely compulsive." A statement which simultaneously referents the beatific twilight of both *Bedouin Hornbook* and *Djbot Baghostus's Run*. The latter creations being riveting circular meditations on the state of the creative nomad, the blend of the writing being of quixotic vertigo. Yes, movement as insubordinate precipitation, where one gets the sense that the "Angel of Dust" does not partake of a separate 3-dimensional realia, but is in fact what Henry Corbin refers to as "unus-ambo," the simultaneity "of the I and the self." The narrator "N" seems to assume the "position of the 'I,'" and the "Angel of Dust" that of the self-image and "mirror"; as Corbin says, "my image looks at me with my own look." And in reading these fictions one gets the sense of another level of converse, outside the call and response of standard literary sculpting. It is a dialogistic taking place within a sphere of interrogative witness, in a zone "no longer day, but not yet night, no longer night, but not yet day." Thus gravity disappears, and is intuitively superseded by a liminal fecundation in which an elliptical nuance of knowledge is extended and evinced. Mr. Mackey converges the "Papyrus of Nesi-Amsu," which is "older than the pyramids," with the "Orquestra Cimmaron" and Jackie McLean. When reading his works the mind feels awash with a shimmering balance of echoes, with a splendiferous ensemble of ghosts in the verbs. The unwieldy, the power of incongruous melody brought to pitch after meandering pitch. It feels like an exquisite intestinal phonation is taking place. And of course, meandering is meant in the manner by which the nomad instinctively navigates movement throughout the sands of eclectic hostility. So the transformative principle which infuses all the situations, all the phrases, all the phonemic subversions, makes up all the encounters, in order to get to the golden rays of insight. In doing so, Mackey shifts to verbal overtone, to the power of written vibrato, witness his verbal painting concerning the "FIVE COMPRESSED ACCOMPANIMENTS TO 'OUR LADY OF THE LIFTED SKIRTS.'" It is lingual movement like an inward ballet, burning in magical unison with itself. Then, there is the inscrutable respiration between "N" and the "Angel of Dust," the latter's voice speaking of a "thinly veiled romance of distantiation"; or the Angel's upwelling questions concerning N's "antithetical opera." Then the mirror spins, and "N" refers to the ancient Egyptian god "Temu" having congress "with himself," thereby producing incandescent offspring. Having said such, it seems to me that "N" and the "Angel of Dust" exist at the fabulous level of mantric self-replication, distinct, but at the same time infused, much in the way that the triple mind communes, the subconsciousness, the consciousness, and the supraconsciousness, all focused at magnetic dusk. His fictions, his poetry, his essays, his readings, course with endogenous conduction, much in advance of those poets content to render their concerns with pedestrian expression.

Of course these are clandestine missives, beatific with intricate whispers, kinetic with tribal telepathy. And though there exist landmarks from recognizable locales, they exist as flecks within the river of insight, and are not influential as gravitative boundaries. No, they serve as connecting points for the "Mystic Horn Society" in their relentless overcoming of consensus immediacy. Each member of the group carries the germ of a regal prestidigitator's poise. The life of the group then naturally exists as a flotational stimulus, as an uprooted flux, as "an ashen finesse."

Attempting these works, one can see that Mr. Mackey's creative largesse is riverine, charismatic. And I stress largesse, because during a prior period of our converse he had expressed to me that during a nascent period of his creativity he had considered himself closer to someone like Robert Creeley in praxis, a clipped, pared down poet, a writer of compressed intuitives. But as accretion of poetic respiration transpired, a leap took place, an extended capability, an efflorescence of stamina, and creations of the multifold and the complex took on enduring precedence. Not only those which include the above mentioned fictions, but also books of poetry, which include Eroding Witness, and School of Udhra. Combine this with his powerful collaboration with musicians the caliber of Hafez Modirzadeh and Royal Hartigan, reading his Songs of the Andoumboulou, as well as conducting the superior skill he exercises as editor of the journal Hambone, and you have an ongoing life performance which clearly transcends the poet as circumscribed polemicist.

When I think of Nathaniel Mackey I am reminded of Mack Thomas's assessment of Eric Dolphy, when he illuminates the latter's philosophical tenor, which in no way hampered his understanding of the specific particulars of the different instruments that he played. As editor, as essayist, as poet, as creator of nomadic epistles, he obliquely illumines the crossroads, with a liminal amperage, not unlike a desert engulfed with elliptical simooms, empowered by the fount of an archetypal Nubia, powerfully irrigating the reader's imaginal plateau, with the ironic current of sustained solar susurration.

ON MERILENE MURPHY

(1956–2007)

Dauntless, bohemian, burning. A surge of fire, poetic quanta. This was Merilene, never for a moment abstracted, or squared in her motion by dispassionate reduction. She possessed that unique understanding of language at its genesis, as primordial conduction. It was as if she were completely subsumed by its aboriginal osmosis speaking in rhythm with the first poets of the earth when they named volcanoes, and rivers, and herons, and stars.

Her speech, unerring charisma, rhythmic circulation, carrying at times a power not unlike an irrational eaglet singing from its perch beneath the light of instantaneous moons.

If one were so lucky to have Merilene as audience, or fellow traveler, or critic, the atmosphere would ignite like blue interior sun magic, her light like the pure interior ardor of the Divine. So when I think of her I can never recall any restriction or limit. She was and remains that charismatic creatrix, whose African rhythmos continues to ring like a ballet of bells from her voice.

FOR LAURENCE WEISBERG

(1952–2003)

To register moment by moment the language of translucence and eruption puts one far beyond the content of the daily wage earner's concerns. One is no longer magnetized as a captured wattage measured by concerns of the marketplace. One burns with telepathic sensitivity, with alchemical non sequitur, one's daily renewal consumed by "hidden number." One then walks on ground "prepared by vast space," like a dazzling but invisible leopard, always kinetic at the cusp of a strange interior daybreak. Such was the odyssey of Laurence Weisberg as he roamed day after day throughout a curious phonemic forest.

He did not carry a day planner, or plot book by book a lucid literary archive, gaining name recognition by sterility. Instead his ink would flare, the images transcend, as a diamond erupting at the borderland of beauty. Certainly not a conservative machination, or a practical polemic aimed at the reader engrossed by popular momentary concern.

Laurence wrote by means of faceless evanescence, his voice seduced by flames of golden lorikeets. Being an intrinsic wanderer, a scribe from the Chaldea of Artaud, Laurence was most at home sitting in dark cafés conjuring up sun dogs, or speaking from interior Oaxacas. This was the level of his work, never offering himself up to quotidian duality, or to the workbench of the critics. Instead he worked from the blueprint of the untouchable, form the "firmament of utopias."

He has now ascended to poetic solar planes where the "ghosts stand erect in their uniforms of fire." Yet he remains amongst us, as dweller alive with beatific concern, his voice illuminate over and above that which is reasonable, unconcerned with the elements praised by conversation and description.

RE-EMERGENCE FROM THE CATACOMBS

When a true poet factors into visibility it is cause for excitement. It is to witness a new condensation of energy, with all its rapture and uniqueness. Not that K. Curtis Lyle has never appeared in print, or given readings, or read his poems in performance with musicians. He has nonetheless hovered in that zone of interjacence, maintaining a profile of fugitive incandescence. There have been poems printed in Quincy Troupe's anthologies *Confrontation* and *Giant Talk*, as well as *Black Digest* and other less chronicled journals, but appearance in print has been rare over the past two decades. His two books, *Drunk On God* and *15 Predestination Weather Reports*, date from the mid-to-late 1970's, and there have been no new books, and nothing I can note concerning individual poems anthologized during this time period. In this regard Lyle has remained a puzzling temperature, especially while writing with prolific concentration over the past decade and a half. Lyle works by the principle that if excellent work is produced, people will find it. This book is living proof of that principle.

His poems partake of both the telluric and the stellar—images erupt in the form of interior code, rhythms are aboriginal, powers partake of ferocious lingual audacity. A philosophical threading blended with subversive humor. In particular, I'm thinking of "Sometimes I Go To Camarillo & Sit In The Lounge," and "The Guerrilla Ecstatics." But if one looks through his whole oeuvre, the poems blaze, and concentrate like heat from concealed scorpions. This is an organic Surrealism where a fish reverses its nature by loving "land" and fearing "water." It is not the subconscious welter of Surrealism as theory, but the ability to blink and see images. It is the Surrealism not of Breton but of Tutuola, without having to move the stubborn weight of conscious mass. Lyle's images seem to naturally form into great nonlinear lists. For instance, when he speaks in one breath of Emiliano Zapata, Bud Powell, Charlie Parker, and Diego Rivera, in the poem "Tampa Red's Contemporary Blues," or the catalogue of hallucinogens in "The Guerrilla Ecstatics." But the poem which struck me the most in this regard was "Poem In Quest Of The Pure Image." Everything was there: the "poisonous stone," the "electricity" of "eels," the "impregnable avocados." It is a poem tireless in its energies with its "mad-orange sun," its "remarkable birds," its "decibel of hyenas." The words explode and fly, and hurl themselves to the earth, while maintaining themselves in a state of simultaneous rotation. Reading the poem made me ecstatic. I realized that it was possible to conduct oneself this way in English. True, I had been in close contact with poems of Bob Kaufman and Philip Lamantia; I had read *The Palm-Wine Drunkard*. But Lyle was someone who had developed in the community in which I lived, in which I was questing for an ecstatic kind of language. I too had the fire of the seeker.

When we finally began conversing I felt doubly blessed, having the privilege of reading his work and conversing with the source. The conversation would take place in his house on odd Thursday or Saturday afternoons, discussing Kaufman, Paz, Césaire, Rabearivello. It was grasping through dialogue the great legacy that informed us. Yet there existed this difference: I occupied a teeming proto-field, but it was Lyle who published his works in the realm of Hernton, Césaire, and Neruda.

By sustaining our conversation over time, language and its reality as imminence began to magnify. I began to absorb this reality, giving me the confidence to take language beyond the pragmatic, the didactic, the plain-spoken. These talks were organic for me; they helped sustain my first roots, growing as they were against the imaginal limitation expected of the Afro-American poet. I had yet to meet Lamantia and Kaufman, so Lyle was the first contact I had with an international rhythmus. He was composing a poem almost daily, which to this day remains an extraordinary sustainment. Witnessing such praxis gave me a double revelation; one: to hone each word, each line by means of the imaginal through intense aural condensation; two: to weave and develop these lines into anomalous interiorized epics. It was during these osmotic exchanges that *Asia & Haiti*, and all the longer compositions I've subsequently penned were originally seeded.

Lyle's poems continue to free us "from the immediate images of perception," allowing us the realization to "absent" ourselves, to "make a leap toward a new life." And this "leap" was manifested by a concomitant social condition in the mid 1970's. At this time both Lyle and myself were members in an extended community which was not unlike the great Surrealist gatherings some sixty years earlier, or the utopian communes evinced by Fourier a century prior to Breton. One of our central hubs was the Broadway and Manchester local where the Los Angeles musicians Ray and Ernest Slaughter operated a collective incense business. In essence it was an Afro-Surrealist hive frequented by poets, musicians, and fellow travelers. Rasul Sadik, Azar Lawrence, Kamau Daáood were spontaneous participants. There were others too numerous to mention. But it burned outside the stratagems of the academy, outside the fact of the rational principle. It peopled a zone that Parker Tyler has called "elsewhere."

This period has gone unnoticed because it remains infortuitous with the media. It is not the Los Angeles of Rodney King, of the Crips and the Bloods, of the Black community as a conclave of crime and drugs. It was and remains a symbol for making great imaginal leaps. It carried on the great Los Angeles tradition of Eric Dolphy, of Charles Mingus, of Ornette Coleman, of Jayne Cortez, of the Watts Writers Workshop, of which Lyle was a founding member. It is the tradition of making magical art through experiment by lightning. Playing with parsecs of salt on the page. More succinctly put, the poetic plane.

And this is where Lyle has remained, on the poetic plane, linguistically prismatic, having passed through both the visible and invisible obstruction poets are wont to endure. You have here poems that have passed through the chrysalis of obstacle, without stuttering, without the crutches of academic encoding, evincing a luminous electrical scent, a music where the rhythm of passion is spoken.

BEAH RICHARDS

(1920–2000)

There are some amongst us who never cease evolving. One can count Beah Richards as being at the core of this elect. Despite being born during a most rabid era of apartheid, she was, by 1948, crafting her acting skill at the Globe Theater in San Diego. This became the seed of her spectacular advance. She made a subsequent appearance at the Yale Repertory Theatre, starring in a production of *The Little Foxes*, which provided her access to Broadway in 1956, where she first appeared in *Take A Giant Step*. Her film debut was made several years later when *Take A Giant Step* was adapted to the screen. What followed was a plethora of victories. The Broadway production of *The Miracle Worker* in 1959, later reprising her role as Viney in the film adaptation of the play. As Sister Margaret she starred in the New York production of James Baldwin's *Amen Corner* in 1965, and two years later worked with Sidney Poitier on two compelling films, *In the Heat of the Night*, and *Guess Who's Coming to Dinner?*, the latter garnering her an Academy Award nomination as best supporting actress. Upon her death Poitier made comment about her striking range, which "accommodated theater, film, television, and the lecture stage." He went on to comment that her power was such that there was never "an actor who ever worked with her who wasn't fed by her energy."

Beah, always blessed with an innate regality was never less than soaring in everything that she touched. "Her acclaimed book of poetry, *A Black Woman Speaks*, published in 1950, became a one-woman show that toured the country." Beah's fruitful association with the late C. Bernard Jackson and the Los Angeles Inner City Cultural Center resulted in her directorial debut, directing Mr. Jackson's *Piano Bar*, and in 1971, writing and starring in her own play, *One Is A Crowd*.

But all of the above only explains the outer rim of her volcano. She 1 was always incessant, seething with exploration. Always searching for the positive force in human experience, she was never afraid of controversy, of seeming contradiction. In this regard she has few parallels in the arts. She brings to mind a Paul Robeson, an Aimé Césaire.

Her life and her acting were not of two separate kingdoms. Early on, she had learned from Frank Silvera, "a new method of acting—the philosophy of being, mortal existence in a perfect state." Her consistency in living was astounding. She organically understood balance. By embracing Buddhism in the mid 1970's she further enhanced this balance, giving her a deeper, more calming respiration, enabling her to embark on a dazzling array of endeavors in the latter part of her life; which included a final Emmy won this past September 1st for her appearance on *The Practice*, as well as her charismatic involvement with Theatre of Hearts/ Youth First as an active board member. This latter involvement blended with her belief that arts education is the opening of human potential most striking in the young person's growth. In one of her most telling quotes she emphasized art as being "the barometer of what it is to be a human being," and that it "may be the only effective answer to our social problems."

Being privileged to be a friend and poetic colleague to Beah during the last year of her life, I will miss her, with her uncanny insight, her stamina, her ebullient scope of thought always pressing for discovery.

SHEILA SCOTT-WILKINSON

"ENCOUNTERING A TIGER
ON A NARROW PATH"

We live in an environment where only the accessible is acknowledged, where deeper rooting goes undiscerned. It seems that Sheila Scott-Wilkinson remains a citizen of the undiscerned like a rooted sorceress, whose achievements continue to echo the invisible.

She ignites in our presence as if hurtled from a voracious interdimensional grasp, but like us all she was spawned on terra firma in the anonymous locale of Aurora, Illinois. It was in the anonymity of Aurora that her prowess in the performing arts began to nascently coalesce. Having felt this fever within she has always stated from childhood that she wanted nothing more than to excel at portrayal.

As the only child in the house she began to imagine in solitude, role playing inside the mind, thereby creating an intuitive momentum for further exploration. Embellishment came in the form of voice and piano instruction, with the aforesaid being culminate in a school production of *The Sound of Music*.

These youthful forays were not of insignificance. They ignited a conduction, which opened another view far beyond Aurora and the provinces. It was at this moment that her family reconnoitered the movement beyond the socioracial constrictions of the States. At 17 she embarked on her journey to Germany without a hard and fast plan, yet never looking back. Initially enrolled in the Frankfurt Conservatory of Music by means of her powerful mezzosoprano voice, the course was set for her evolvement to grand opera, yet this was not enough to hold her, seeing as she saw the racial politics of Germany, with its awkwardly devised suppression of its infamous Hitlerian epoch.

In hindsight it stands as her first initiation into the realm of a spectacular nomadics. After two years she broke with the grand opera, leaving this promising venture to explore the peculiar uncertainties of the stage. This latter adventure meant England, where she was accepted at Yat Mamgren's prestigious London Drama Centre, which was followed by performances at The Royal Court, the West End, the Liverpool Playhouse, and the National Theatre. Albee, Arrabal, Bullins, Shakespeare were some of the zones she relentlessly inhabited. Look at the range: *Celestina* by Fernando de Roja, Webster's *Duchess of Malfi*, Albee's *Who's Afraid of Virginia Woolf*, *AC/DC* by Heathcote Williams, *The Homecoming* by Harold Pinter, *The Map of the World* by David Hare. And the aforementioned only tally a small amount of her tremendous activity. She was called by the critic Beryl Jones "an electrifying actress, an irresistible force, like encountering a tiger on a narrow path." Vanessa Redgrave deemed her one of the best actresses in Britain. There was a continuous quality in the energy of her portrayals, quite the opposite of the short term sensibility which disintegrates in the very heat of popular conveyance.

Contemporaneous with Helen Mirren, it was Scott-Wilkinson along with Mirren who blazed the way with the empowering roles which so magically graced the feminine gender. There was her powerful portrayal in the Columbia movie *National Health, or Nurse Norton's Affair* written by Peter Nichol, and on British TV as the reporter Judy Marshall in the series *Diamond Crack Diamond*, as well as the series *Special Branch*. She continued to rivet on screen as she had done on the stage. Add to this her starring presence in Horace Ove's *Pressure*, which was the first black feature film in Great Britain, and you have here a spectacular oeuvre fed by an intuitive volcanics.

Yet American audiences have been cheated of her wonders. Why? When she returned to the States none of the powers in cinema or television would either believe or embrace her achievements. Because of her power she left producers and directors with carking puzzlement in her wake. What was left were those ethnically driven roles which offered no challenge or conflict. Because of her color she was never cast in any role of riveting significance. A stunning case of racial politics.

After a strenuous transition she left the limitations of the screen world before going on to found Theatre of Hearts Youth First. It is a powerful organization which irrigates the imagination of underserved, at-risk youth in Los Angeles County with the arts. As Founder/Director she brings an emboldened tempo to its mission. To date her organization has seeded over 100,000 youth with visual art, with storytelling, with poetry, dance, theater, and music.

In her latest endeavor she has invaded the realms of the photographic, taking pictures of arresting seismography not unequal to the quality that she brought to her previous endeavors on stage and screen. With unprecedented tenor she has injected through the praxis of her presence a penetrating view which helps us extend the powers of the mind.

JOHNNY SEKKA

PARAGON OF THE IMMACULATE (1934–2006)

There are beings who appear in this life through seeming conjuration, whose energy seems to translate through poetic quanta. Of course, they are not without dates, not without the terms which conduct the flow of a biography or chronicle. The biography in Sekka's case conjoins in concert with a destiny over and beyond the sum of his dates and peregrinations. Therefore, his dates and peregrinations were from the moment of his birth invaded by an intriguing stellar charisma.

He first appeared on terra firma July 21st, 1934. The locale was Dakar, capital of Senegal. As one of five siblings he was born into a family at the bottom of the social structure. When his father unexpectedly passed away poverty was compounded, so he was sent with his sister to live with an aunt in Gambia. Early on the otherworldly invaded. His sister was attacked and eaten by crocodiles. He was left as a devastated and singular presence. And this event was more pointedly exacerbated by the ongoing treatment of an aunt who could only abuse his efforts as if performed by an annoying underling.

After unsuccessful attempts at escape, he bided his time finding work "at the docks, where he kept the monkeys off the peanut mountains . . ."

A short time later he escaped by stowing away on a ship to Marseille. With a magnetic French in hand it made movement through French society bearable. But for him France was no stopping point.

By means of his hard-won insight he began casting light on England, moving there in the early 1950's. By 1954 he had met the "well known British actor Earl Cameron" who served "as an early mentor." For Cameron, it was Sekka's ability to mimic people which impressed him so strongly. From this impetus Johnny began "interviewing around London," being eventually "hired as a stage hand for the Royal Court Theatre." This led to "bit parts on stage." Early in the next decade he was recognized as being part of a noteworthy collective which included Michael Caine, John Osborne and Sean Connery. Early on the British press began drawing comparisons between his emerging body of work and that of Sidney Poitier.

What followed was contact by Broadway. Never one to turn down a challenge, he charged across the waters with writer Tony Richardson. But he was thwarted in his debut. The production in question was the musical *Kwamina*. Johnny was told before embarking upon performance that under no circumstance was he allowed to touch his female costar, who was white. Both writer and actor withdrew from the project and it was not until six years later that the stage world relented concerning Sekka and the chronic condition of barrier by color. He was cast as the lead in the stage play of Bakke's *Night of Fame*. Considered the best actor for the role, it was the first time in English theater that a Black actor had been given a role outside the confinement of color.

There were major roles that followed on screen, which included *Master of the Game*, and the controversial *Mohammed, Messenger of God*.

But these latter endeavors and the aforementioned odyssey could never adequately particularize five decades of unbroken achievement in plays, and musicals, and films.

Having met him in his later years, what struck me most about him was the regality of his bearing. And listening to him speak was like entering the zone of utopian enunciation. And I am told this did not solely encompass the dulcet weavings of his English, but was also evident in his French, and in the music of his native Wolof.

What I'm proposing here is a revisitation of his spirit by committed artists of all persuasions. Artists who have risen by means of imagination into a psychic space beyond the quotidian condition as fate. Therefore it is in this space that one can conjoin with the spirit of Sekka, who even in death continues to conspire with the fabulous.

THE FOOTNOTES EXPLODED

FOR BOB KAUFMAN (1925–1986)

A voyager arriving in a darkened opal port, his verbal lenses honed by an ingrown verbal preciseness, by an absence of buried mechanics. I think of the nascent Kaufman inwardly floating through explosive anonymities, never once singed by mundane repetition or sequel. His hearing is replete at the level of intuitive terminology, at the root of its most seminal spinning. His language, part aurora and lava flowing from a central vitrescence. It partakes of the spell, being hypnotic and genetic in demeanor. I mean, there is insight into life which sustains itself by means of intrinsic purity, by means of necessitous obscurity, which can never be subject to rational decoding, to exoteric decipherment. Language then is not a given, not a sum to be captured and examined under prevalent electron regalia. Verbal obstacle then leaps, the accessible as sense, the quotidian as assumption.

By his electrical presence Kaufman's language escapes the analytical, the moment by moment vacuum deemed climatic according to a precedent assumed by the rules of a rational exegesis. And such exegesis denies, and destroys the spontaneous in favor of pattern. Again Kaufman, not a deleted fuchsia, but original respiration. A voice capable of traversing acres of fire, his mandibles torched by elemental tattoos, by various interior grails. And what compels such attention is his superior analogical power aged by a fabulous turbulence. As if he had been cast into frictive waters at the center of a brimstone mountain. It is a poetic energy which continues to prevail, and by prevailing I mean sustained hypnosis as experienced by the reader.

When I first encountered the poem, "To My Son Parker Asleep In The Next Room," an urgency, a vortex occurred within me, as if awakened to a new viridity. Not an exaggeration for a nascent poet to experience, especially one instinctively seduced by subconscious dioramas. It is a writing seemingly soaked by a surreptitious light from a vacated sun. Then reading poems like "SHEILA," "UNHISTORICAL EVENTS," "BLUE SLANTED INTO BLUENESS," became for me like obscure motions spinning in a transfixed carbon house. I was magnetically engulfed.

As Kaufman poetically appeared with his broadsides he was already of seminal import, he was already the nizam, the rajah. According to the photographer Jerry Stoll, Kaufman was a "pioneer," a "functioning . . . critic of society," "much more social and political . . . than any of the other poets in North Beach . . ."[1] He carried his own migrational light which led people like Ginsberg into a greater activists' capacity. In this regard, Kaufman was the proto-source, the engendered proto-Sphinx, who simply appeared without formal literary precedent, much in the manner of Lautréamont or Rimbaud. Of course this is plain to us now, but in the atmosphere of the 1950's, with the case against the Rosenbergs still hissing, with the rasping carcinogens of McCarthy generally rife throughout the atmosphere, he showed unprecedented character. General threat corroded the foreground; metropolitan areas swarmed with informers, all enigmas were suspected. Non-condoned behavior was thought of as allergic, as partaking of treasonous errata. And Kaufman at this moment was the inscrutable lightning rod, possessed of courage and greenish defiance, who transmuted life into sound, into supernal ensembles of magic verbal liquid.

His "flaming water," his "Indian suicides,"[2] capable of conversing with a box of amoebas, capable of "shining" on "far historical peaks."[3] Kaufman in this register remains eminently uncontainable. In this he literally embodies the surreal in that not a single line is operatically planned or thought out as regards publishable criteria. But upon reading his work, levels of intensity are not lacking, nor is a spectacular use of oral language convened to suicidally incinerate the printed page with aleatoric detachment. No, the language remains powerful in book form, fused in its leaps by antisedentary scorching. Yet Kaufman seemed to swelter with an inborn hostility to literature and its sustained identity in the reductive. Because of this, his verbal tremblings remain profuse with usurption and voltage as he acknowledged "the demands of surrealist realization," as he challenged "Apollinaire to stagger drunk from his grave and write a poem about the Rosenbergs' last days" while smouldering in the "Death House."[4]

Where do we find lines like Kaufman's in the present poetic American pantheon; lines stunning with irregular galvanic, with endogenous wingedness, with relentless surprise?

In the surge of Lamantia there are parallels, there are moments in Corso and Crane, in the visions of Daniel Moore, which synaptically lurk in the ricochets of his concussive charisma. He remains ulterior, clandestine, in the way his verbal cancellations deduct their actions in crossing subversive esplanades. And he poetically protracts this vapor across dialectical respiration being "eternally free in all things."[5] He spoke of Java, of "Melanesian mountain peaks,"[6] of Assyria's "earthen dens,"[7] of Camus as "sand faced rebel from Olympus."[8] So Kaufman continues to exist for me like a verdigris Phoenix, arising and re-arising from the poets' ill-begotten lot even as he smoulders "in a cell with a view of evil parallels."[9]

The quintessential scion of chance linguistic praxis, Kaufman's poems continue moment by moment to irradiate electricity. Continue within the range of immaculate verbal searing, spun from green elliptical finery.

Saying this, do I place Kaufman on a pedestal just to celebrate him in death, to claim inspiration from the sum of abstract mirage? I can answer without hesitation, no. During the early 1980's I would travel to North Beach as towards some internal Mecca, wandering its labyrinths in and out of enclaves. These illusive glimpses were like poetic talismans for me, sparks of gold in the labyrinth. I would always see him on angles from a distance, and near the end of one auric afternoon we stood face to face at oblique remove, and I called out his name, and at the evaporation of his name from my lips he literally vanished into one of the teeming dives in the vicinity of Vallejo. Which immediately brought to mind the parallel of Pessoa and his spontaneous disappearance during his walks across Lisbon.

During this period he lived adjacent to Philip Lamantia. And it was one morning after emerging from a dozen hour dialogue with the latter, that we walked across Harwood Alley to Neely Cherkovski's who tended Kaufman during those days. It was about 8 A.M. one Monday morning, and Kaufman remained sequestered in the other room, as both of us peered at the original typewritten manuscript of "The Ancient Rain." I

mention this episode because both Kaufman and Lamantia have had instantaneous impact upon my poetic formation. Have made foray after
foray into my hermetically sealed lingual athanor, and their verbal osmotics continue to seep into my imaginal ozone, letting me know moment after moment that imaginal radiance can prevail.

In discussing Kaufman, all academic insertion is passionately de-
clined; is ravaged, with all its footnotes exploded. The contours blurred,
the circumferences alchemically splayed by the beauty of mathematical
absence. And I mean mathematics in its lower form, in its niggling ban-
ter concerning the petty matter of equated equidistance.

When poets sought shelter beneath an academic archway, Kaufman
assaulted police, and was arrested more than 30 times in a single year.
When poets sought for the proper form to ensconce their subject matter,
Kaufman wrote of "UNHOLY MISSIONS," of "HEATHER HELL," of the
previously mentioned "SHEILA," "CAST OUT OF RAINCLOUDS ... ON
WARPED FADED CAROUSELS." The verbal structures collapse and revi-
sualize, not in terms of a furtive literary comment, nor as ironic line sustained by the pressure of brilliantly acceptable wit. Kaufman's language
condenses to aboriginal ubiquity, being that status of poet who heard his
words as untranslated molten, like an abnormal eaglet deciphering his
reptilian forerunners with intangible preciseness; the sound spun by "il-
lusionary motion,"[10] by the liquor of exploded roses, blazing as quantum
mass beyond the reasoned scope of antideracination.

A poet who followed his own endogenous helical road, roaming
through "vacant theaters,"[11] erasing "taxable public sheets."[12] Kaufman
so derealized the archives, that he negated all rational effort by sifting
through auricular winds of dialectical transparency, thereby mining an
inevitable verbal aurum. The three dimensions magnificently destabi-

lized and fleetingly focused like "tall strips of carrion moonlight sparing only stars."[13] Thus he occupied a seditionary grammatical bastion, implying "a horror of trades."

He knew like Rimbaud, that "the hand that guides the pen is worth the hand that guides the plow."[14] Thus, he threw routine and stasis into the quarrelsome antidotes of debris.

And even in death, Kaufman continues to magically advance across a blinding reticular sea, without the mercator's imprisoning symmetrics, electric with utopias, far outside the parochial reportage of mechanical matching burins, poised as they are against the pure fluidity of desire.

Of course, Kaufman refuses to match, to sustain the subject of "conferences" à la Kerouac and Ginsberg, so crucially pointed out by Maria Damon. He continues to exist "beyond official Beat history,"[15] beyond its canon as inscribed by the Whitney Museum, beyond the delineated form of the countercultural figure within the scope of defined exotic boundary. No, there is a more sustained projection from his blood, which at present remove naturally leaps the specific mercury of a bygone era, transcending its once arresting intent, spiraling into an expanded counterrotation, which occupies the poets' true domain, which Parker Tyler on another occasion deemed the interior kingdom of "Elsewhere."

AT
PENULTIMATE
REMOVE

A NOTE ON ALLEN
GINSBERG (1926–1997)

I never saw him at Sausalito or Innsbruck, surrounded by the tentacles of Myrmidons, but at the optimum remove of touch, while operant as a momentary colleague during his last active summer at Naropa. Whether we conversed over repast, or did mutual signings of our books together, I always found him gracious, with an energy always giving of itself, an energy never abstracted, or overly rational with delay.

I remember the final Friday of my stay, engulfed by a bright unblemished Colorado sky, and the Colloquia that day when the students engaged the total Faculty in dialogue. I could feel Allen taking on instant rapport with the audience, his basic instincts still alert, although I could feel the shadows seep from his body like a caliginous osmotics. There was palpable decline, yet his protean appetite for life continued to activate, continued to cast living signs upon the wind. Though the vector which enlivened him during earlier times seemed less rapt, it nevertheless emitted its presence like wintry solar flare, condensing all the lives within his life, already suggesting emission of its rays into a transmuted after life. And as I conclude on these bits, these limited sparks of conversation, I can only feel fortunate to have graced the presence of one whom many have sought to emulate and transcribe from bastions from afar.

PHILIP LAMANTIA

PERPETUAL INCANDESCENCE (1927–2005)

Philip Lamantia even in surcease, remains that omnivorous presence which continues to proliferate a state of perpetual incandescence. Not a state empowered by personality or anecdote, but a cryptic state of perpetual attainment. Such attainment is especially difficult to appreciate given that its vocabulary remains alchemical, recondite, disassociated from the grounded terrain of the accessible view.

This is why the standard obituary can never take into account that which rises above the monomial view of dates and places, with its acceptable resume of encounters.

This is not the context to list the specifics of a debilitated aunt, or chronicle mazes of poverty, or bring to the fore a pointless educational compendium. Philip Lamantia does not inspire a resurrection of relics. What can be evinced from his sojourn on earth are those unforgettable comminglings of language which partake in their motion incipient utopias. Utopias where glass fissions, where rainbows transmute to migration by birds.

I recall in this momentary glare three transcendental figments from Philip's biography; Andre Breton, the "Cora Indian tribe at Nayarit," his hermetic embrace of the ozone and its birds. In the first case he receives the password from a magus; in the second case he resurrects from the ashes; in the third case he returns whole sole and body to the unity of the cosmos.

This transpires over a period of 40 years. But a 40 years outside the climate as we've come to know it under quotidian occupation. For Philip it was to absent himself from the claustrophobia of time, to reach into an interior cataclysmic not unlike the imaginal radiance evinced by Gaston Bachelard. The "double meaning," the metaphor, the shift in planes. Language as superior kinetic by analogy.

So Philip palpitates, poem after poem, book after book, like quantum spiraling, intermittent, oblique, fueled by the sun of interjacence. Not the sun as furnace, but light as transformative eternity.

And it was this great impersonal fire which first dazzled me about Lamantia. His works became my cryptic ritual criteria. I was always listening to him in my mind, and so when I met him face to face it was a twelve-hour encounter which has marked me forever. He being the saturated icon, the onyx bird who knew the invisibility of knowledge and its power beyond reason.

He knew electrical vivacity through hearing. The poet for him was conduit, was transmuted fever imbued by the grammar of superior integrity. And it is from this integrity that he knew true community is restored.

We remain saddened by the absence of his magical vehicular presence, yet his language, and the tenacity of his vigil will always inspire us as we enter the Mayan mental calendric, with new fuels in the cells, where the human species can commence concert with expanded being, over and beyond our present solar locality in the cosmos.

THE WING OF IMAGINAL

AFRICAN ANTIGRAVITY

DIASPORA, NÉGRITUDE, BLUES

ABOVE A MARRED POETIC ZODIAC AND ITS CONFINES

. . . a metaphysics of the unforgettable.

—GASTON BACHELARD

The reality now accrues concerning the poets' leap beyond marred verbal zones of pedestrian psychic levels, beyond their antitransgressives, beyond their skittish colloquial internment.

How is such intensity exerted?

By the high power of sustained imaginal exuberance like a blur of alchemical eagles over peaks. Such is the movement of a seamless astral sonar eclipsing the power of tedious linguistics. The latter condones work as institutional commandment, as imperial ballast raised to an insidious level, falsely evolved beyond miraculous Hottentot cyclonics. But perpendicular poetry empowers insight by escaping the ferment of Euroglobal suicide, surreptitiously taking up sides with the billion plus kinetics we call life on terra firma. But eclipse of this kinetic is stored in the stinging anticells manufactured in the despicable blue prints found in the radioactive archives of a distracted G-7 death house. Life in such an enclave has taken on a post-Christian paralysis, where the northern nations speak of omegas if they cannot continue to prevail over the 4 billion wanderers who hover in the heated southern cone of the planet. Inwardly carnivorous, waiting for the abyss to swallow the desires of a dying linear dénouement, this linear motive now having fallen to a pervasive antibiotic which vies with its own obstruction, neutered in its quest for a superior method.

Outmoded ytterbium, fatal nuclear soils in transition.

At bottom, the northern nations wish that plutonium could follow a predirected path so that only the aboriginals were prone to its vapors. The subtraction of the Caribbean people and their dust, the extraction from life of the Blackened Uruguayan ethos, and its resonance throughout the world in parts of Panama or Puerto Rico. This is the suasion of the northern world at its most desperate. Presently it is moribund, it chatters like an old man in odd daylight slowly sipping on his last remaining bottles of vitality. In contradistinction, what suddenly comes to life for me are the maroons, the Seminoles, the renegade Apaches. The rebellious genes in the blood. The scorpion-like resistance of Campana, the thesis of Césaire's *Discourse*, the Paz of "The Broken Water Jar," Peret, with his deadly bursts against structure. This is the power Garcia Lorca was imbued with, flying like a ravenous eagle through the structures of Manhattan. This was New York with its hardened divisions, pinioned with piecemeal and torment. As he pens in "The King of Harlem":

> Ay Harlem! Ay Harlem! Ay Harlem!
> There is no anxiety comparable to your oppressed scarlets
> to your blood shaken within your dark eclipse,
> to your garnet violence deaf and dumb in the penumbra,
> to your great King, a prisoner with a commissionaire's uniform.[1]

Words which reflect the gall so soaked in his vision of a haughty imperialist schooner sailing around the planetary mind with its leaking official kinetic. Now the schooner continues to float under the powers of an enigmatic turpitude, claiming distance from its crimes, its lying, its historicity of betrayal, claiming a shaken distance from actions which have ransacked whole blood lines.

Against this invidious backdrop there seems to be a rigid American festering as regards conducting such subjects in its poetry. I am thinking of the poetic Anglophones, who, from the beginning of the Modernist era have not significantly evolved beyond language in the service of a mental colonialist's hegemony. Only E. A. Robinson with his monological "Toussaint L'Ouverture" allows a natural meteoritic to erupt beyond the throes of the stereotypic, of the inferior guise of the Black man as simian. Therefore he refutes the Jeffersonian Black bestiality as a given, forcing us "away from the Steinian assumptions of the earthiness of the black and causes us to consider the nonwhite 'as more than a transplanted shovelful / Of black earth, with a seed of danger in it.'" Robinson gives vivacity to Toussaint, letting him carry the blood of his own dignified battalions. He has not attempted to reduce the solar forces in his nature; instead, he has let them speak, unlike the intense deformities of Pound, with his toxic mood swings towards Africa. Saying such, let us reel in the whole Modernist menagerie. Williams, Eliot, Cummings, Stevens, all linguistic subfeeders to the dominant racial mind set of the day. In their ethos hovered the stone of state-sponsored ideology. At their lowest they serve as promulgators of the incalculable double holocaust of the Indians, and the Africans transported across the stench of shark-filled slaved waters. At this lowest pitch I find in Cummings mere typographical innovation, in Pound, a robber of universal graveyards. Outside of Aldon

Nielsen's impressive uncoverings there has never been a consistent pointing to their moral ineptitude and cowardice. The non-white exists for this lot as a splotch of local color, subsequently scattered like a darkened salt throughout the angles of their world renowned tropes. So, this Latinization that Eliot called for is merely the breeding of icons transparently hidden beneath colonialistic Christianity.

Can one see Pound or Cummings welcoming Aimé Césaire into the world of letters circa 1941? No, this could never have happened, from those who culturally reeked of the spoils of the former plantation builders—safe, brazen, deluded, much like the writing of Cummings when he dons his many minstrel masks. So when Breton singles out Césaire as a "Great Black Poet," he is simply balancing reality, he is putting conviction to the test, racing through the pressure like a blue-white diamond, the sun being seen in its substance no longer imbued with a passionless racial ice. He finds in Césaire a man who extinguishes the Greco-Roman as sole unbroken authority. In contrast to Breton, someone like Eliot would never publicly acknowledge that it was the Moors, and not the scholars of the Renaissance, who saved Euripides and the Greeks from premature oblivion. But Blacks in this philosophical machinery are at best given the identity of oarsmen, of objects to be laughed at, to be spat upon. The very nature of the voice as renegade, of interrogator of the state, is missing. The whole Modernist school, even as it reaches through to Ginsberg and O'Hara, with the latter's early imagery, "indicative of his wholesale adoption of the stereotypes of high modernism; indicative also of a willingness to think of the mass of " Black "people as an abstraction to be acted on."

When poets of such stature fail to challenge the mores of a brutally dense racial blemish, their audacity decreases, their images desperately weaken and precipitously descend into a state-condoned subtext. There exists during the 1930's and 40's no sustained poetic attack against a Prussian-like apartheid, against the unbroken pact of the lynch law. Where, in such praxis can one find the moral equivalent of Breton? In Vachel Lindsay's "The Congo," in Stevens' "The Greenest Continent?" Hardly. They are at best excuses in assumption and safety. It is an isolated world, closed, turned in on itself. But because all worlds breathe, it carries its dialectical respiration. On the one hand, there is Eliot strutting in his Anglican métier, and Willliams with his colloquial insight into the "American Grain," but to both, the non-white always objectified, always considered as a trinket, as an exotic marsupial. Can one imagine them denouncing the American occupation of Haiti in the way, say, that the Surrealists denounced the French-Moroccan war in 1925? On the contrary, Stevens during this period praises the likes of Mussolini, and accedes him his right to envelop Ethiopia in the way that he sees fit.

When such actions are compared to poets such as Javier Heraud, and Otto René Castillo, the academicians should tear up their notes and new assessments be considered. Heraud "was a Peruvian who died at 21 while fighting in the jungles of his native country, under the banner of the Liberation Front." Castillo "was active in Guatemalan resistance from the age of 17 . . . imprisoned, tortured, exiled various times during his short life, finally returned to Guatemala . . . for the last time late in 1966." He fought "under the late Major Turcios Lima, and in March, 1967" was captured by anti-guerilla forces "after 15 days of eating nothing but roots." On the 19th of March, "after four days of brutal torturing," they burned him alive. To some, these latter examples may partake of extremity, but the points I'm making have to do with stamina, with courage, with the ability to make do with honed linguistic defiance.

What is lacking in the Modernists, and many of their present day practitioners, is the power of imaginal radiance, leaping "toward a new life." The images for the most part are gravid, psychically patrolled, harnessed within the expedient realm of the generally expected. A conservation of language, so as to court in the long run the empirical perception, the accessible intelligibility, more in keeping with prosaic factors of journalistic dossiers. So when the image comes to me of

> The mandrake horse
> electrically pounding
> the surf of the stars

I feel immediacy, the exuberance of feeling the verbal field on fire. In consequence, it puts me at odds with those poets who "have given us a massive literature of sensibility," of "self narration," of "literal confessions." And what I am speaking of is "pragmatic" usage in service of the cult of reputation. Bachelard says, "To acquire a feeling for the imaginative role of language, we must seek, in every word, the desires for otherness, for double meaning, for metaphor . . . we must record all the desires to abandon what we see and what we say for what we imagine. We shall then have some chance of restoring to the imagination its role of attraction. To perceive and imagine are antithetic as presence and absence."[2]

The colloquial chauvinism against which he speaks is found in Berryman's *The Dream Songs*, seen in the second poem of the volume, where he conjures an "oneiric minstrel show," which would have brought much joy to the heart of Edwin P. Christy, founder of insulting blackface performance circa 1842. Nothing more than invidious grounding, nothing more than a pragmatic stereotype dressed up in the form of a dream. As for me, I agree with Césaire "That 2 and 2 make 5," that my "voodoo brews are stronger"[3] than the confused and overrated spillage of *The Cantos*.

As Sri Aurobindo has so rightly stated, the zodiac is bounded, and can only carry in its seduction a partial awareness of what the greater life can be. This could be said with the previous American literary era in mind, with its racist agrarian zodiac, which attempted to isolate its beacon, taking no account of larger imaginal possibility, excluding the nocturnal with consciously distributed objects, the stereotypic ideal preferred over the squalls of high uranian music, its language explicitly embedded in its suffocating signals formed by dysfunctional perception.

THE CARIBBEAN

LANGUAGE AS TRANSLUCENT IMMINENCE

Language, being the primal conductor of liberty, becomes the magnetic barometer of the primary link between the salubrious psyche and the world in which it exists. It carries in its wake a fervor, a confidence, a pronation, like a perpetual monsoon tree dialectically consumed and utopian, so that bondage to an inferior magnetic is broken and one is freed to explore the linguistic realms protracted through the turbulence of one's identity. And in the Caribbean identity has been none other than the suppressed African content of speech. The deprecated rotation, the subtractive kinetic, continuously devitalized by the Metropolitan psyche as it advances its tenets from London, or Amsterdam, or Paris.

In the Caribbean, the slavers' most lasting form of power has been their hold over language, their mesmeric dispensation to the African diaspora concerning the latter's collective debasement, and their status at the bottom of the human order. The French, the Dutch, the English, the Spanish, from the first debacle of capture, brutally imparted a psychophysical alienation upon the African identity, so that every person of color was haunted by a definitive self-hatred. One's identity was then controlled by values which effectively inscribed upon the mind a piacular and incontrovertible image combined by failure, alienation, and barbarity. One's self assertion was thereby withdrawn, and no reason or ambition could persist. One was simply a tool to be used to the greater good of a European economy based upon one's neglect and impalement.

So when these standards were thoroughly internalized and repetitively recodified, generations emerged replete with self-imposed doubt, crippled by a punitive self-stalling negation. One then exists by means of alien definitives, by charismatic benchmarks, which label one's worth as the lessser darker property, capable of occupying nothing more than the level of a despicable, nefarious misfit. A contemptible adjective incapable of possessing a necessitous moral vigor, which would spur one's self-governing ability.

In consequence, there is always instruction from the racial elite as regards how best to tailor one's day to day needs, restricted as they are to the sullen discord of the bestial. Injustice becomes one's daily metier carried out with the blessing of a hierarchy condoned by the Judeo-Christian deity.

Under such circumstance all stamina is tested in every hamlet of occupation, be it Monserrat or Barbados or Gudeloupe, all possessions of greater Europe. Therefore, what the person of color represents is what the Cuban Retamar calls "the culture of Caliban." "Caliban is thus the fear-object and savage slave of the Western psyche, the dream-evil that terorrizes the night play of timid, fair-skinned Western children."[1] As George Lamming puts it: "Caliban is excluded, that which is eternally below possibility and always beyond reach. He is seen as an occasion, a state of existence which can be appropriated and exploited for the purposes of another's own development. Caliban is a reminder of lost virtue or the evil vigor of the Beast that is always there: a magnetic temptation, an eternal warning against the contagion of his daemon ancestry." Lamming continues, profoundly understanding that "Caliban should be embraced as the continuing possibility of a profound revolutionary change initiated by Toussaint L'Ouverture in the Haitian war of independence."2

So by making a leap, by embracing one's African eclipse sun, one casts out the ideal of Metropolitan acculturation, moving in harmony with an inner African rhythm, no longer naively ingesting facts which Césaire mocks, such as the reign of "Queen Blanche of Castile," or say, in an English speaking confine, being subject to such niggling datum as the death of Queen Victoria and the accession of Edward the VIIth to the throne. Such details become negligible, obsolescent, to be kicked about like a dishonored corpse over stones.

Of course, such previous assertion has not always been the case. Say I were a British subject in Barbados at the beginning of the 1930's. I would in no way understand the seminal undermining of Toussaint's Haiti by Western trade blockade. I would subconsciously attribute Toussaint's failure to the darkness of his integument, which would equate in my mind with an inherent lack of stewardship. I would then look into the mirror and confirm my thesis by the impoverished state of my own self-esteem. Self-defeat acknowledged, my understanding would only range to the region's superficial historicity. I could account for the settlement of Barbados by the English in 1627; I could mention in passing that Monserrat was christened by Columbus and colonized by Irish settlers in 1632; or inadvertent lucidity would bring forth the fact that in 1648 Saint Martin was partitioned by the French and the Dutch. As to any intrinsic speculation concerning revolt or defiance, none would occur. Nothing in the neural field would vibrate, my electric nest of spiders would condense in self-imposed blankness. No psychic concurrence with the blood of Dahomey, with the miraculous powers of Timbuktu.

So when Césaire breaks away from mulatto saloons in Paris, and concentrates in linguistic return to high Africa the aforedescribed scenario is irreparably rent by means of a ferocious seditionary language, by means of intense verbal scaupers, tearing down the veneer of the complexity of self-hatred, so what emerges from his Antillean powers is the "turbulent poetry" of magnetic cyclone trees. He then rings by means of language the bell of self-contact, thereby connecting the visible with the invisible, conspicuity with concealment. By means of the dialectic he becomes capable of mining an African neural eden where purpose and meaning are electrically revealed, empowered by flames of vertiginous fecundity. Melanin then becomes psychophysical empowerment no longer squared by Eurocentric distortion. When, like Césaire one comes to such interior fruition one no longer fields dictates from the British or the French concerning the depth of one's telluric designation.

Yet the point is well taken when Siméa, mother of principal narrator Marie-Gabriel, "remonstrates with Suzanne Césaire" in Daniel Maximin's novel, *Lone Sun*. Seeing her native Guadeloupe in the same degree as she does her neighbour Martinique, she finds fault with Madame Césaire for so heavily consulting Frobénius, a "white ethnologist" on things African. But Siméa or other critics must understand that a start was made in the Tropiques, an African motor principle was acknowledged. Yes, a certain threshold was crossed, a certain amplitude was heightened as regards the African diaspora and the nobility of its origin.

From the genesis of this fortuitous spark, it became possible to open to the homocentric context of ancient Ghana, of Songhai, of Mali. By such opening as Négritude provided there was organic access to, say, the mathematical and astronomical genius of the Dogon people. Black people who "knew of the rings of Saturn," of "the four principle moons of

Jupiter," of "the rotundity of the earth and its turning on its axis."3 And at a more astounding pitch they knew of the "intricate details of the Sirius star system," of its "white dwarf companion star," of Sirius's approximate mass, its orbital period, also its period of axial rotation. And this is knowledge known for at least five hundred years. Five hundred years throughout which the European propagandists have berated the African mind as having procured no intrinsic achievement. We are told by this spurious assumption that peoples such as the pygmies of the Ituri Forest were at the opposite pole of human sensibility. Yet it has been revealed that they knew of nine moons of Saturn without any recourse to modern instrumentation. It becomes naturally understood that use of one's own language provides an illuminant umbilical connecting the past to the crucial complexities of the future.

What the future represents are voices, like the just mentioned Daniel Maximin, or Edouard Glissant, or the many times famous Franz Fanon. They create a tenor for the person of color to make an orphic descent into and out of the "pit of interiority" so as to recover and facilitate a Black psychic force, thereby dissolving by this movement alienation as given. So from this orphic act, a surge transpires in which European classification takes on the character of a disrupting anomaly. For this reason there is now the uncontested ability of the Caribbean writer to take this liberty as given, where one is no longer "thought by others." Language becomes a heritage of complexity, not a mechanical placement of steps, but infused by a perplexity of plenitude, in which to be "part European does not necessarily mean to be assimilated, to lose one's racial and cultural identity." Thus the Antillean personality ceases to reel within the throes of a peripheral cul-de-sac, with suppositious values drawn from pernicious incitement. And this pernicious incitement promulgated by European inhibition, which sees the mind as the last battlefield of suggestion.

In this too the former colonizers have in the long term failed. Take the collective quote from the Antillean writers Jean Bernabé, Patrick Chamoiseau, and Raphaël Confiant, who state that:

> It was Césaire's Négritude that opened to us the path or the actuality of
> a Caribbeanness which from then on could be postulated, and which it-
> self is leading to another yet unlabelled degree of authenticity. Césairen
> Négritude is a baptism, the primal act of our restored dignity. We are
> forever Césaire's sons.

And even if the critic Bernadette Cailler criticizes Daniel Maximin's *Lone Sun* for failing to achieve the combination between 'poetry and history' I think one can safely say that the book would not carry its present predilection were it not for the pioneering bravery of the poets Dumas and Césaire. By their acts the Rubicon of "intellectual poverty" was crossed, putting language in contact with the "primordial," with the "multivalent."

By plunging into orphic turbulence Césaire withdrew his words from utilitarian usage, thereby "disalienating them and restoring ... to his Black people, their original state of possibilities, their state of 'virtualité'" Because of this all things persist in the connivance of liberty. The flora, the fauna, the lyrical botany of the atmosphere can be described as a "perfectly green sea" under "a prodigious orange light." The tellurian powers take on an enthralling force of grammar, where tornadoes cast spells, where the native gecko takes on the power of a noctambulant radiance.

The Antilles, truly south of the American South, where unlike the diaspora to the north, its inhabitants at present both enjoy a psychic, as well as numerical advantage. And it exists for me as a hidden ark for both present and future African concatenation, from which a beacon transpires, mesmerically burning with the stars of a translucent imminence.

A FUGITIVE NOTE ON HAITI

The source of Africa within the Western ethos. Its incipience transmuted a threefold horror: the Arawaks' slaughter by the Spanish; the initial plantations spawned by pirates from the Cayman Islands; the brutality of Saint Dominique under the slave codes of the French.

As Saint Dominique it was a hellish misnomer shadowed in saturnine obliqueness, marked by drudgery and blood, being a trenchant source of unmarked graves.

The inferno we know as Haiti was sparked in 1791 when two mulatto freedmen were butchered for crossing to Paris, petitioning the powers therein concerning the rights of their darker brethren. Oge and Chavannes were the principals whose drawn and quartered bodies were hung at a Saint Dominique crossroads upon their returning, their corpses serving as brutal warning to both freedman and slave. But rather than inspire repression this event ignited Boukman and Toussaint, and from Boukman and Toussaint there erupted Dessalines and Christophe. The result, the routing of the French from its confines. It was a victory of Africa over the West. From Rochambeau to Jefferson, 1804 marked the year that the incumbent dermatology of the West was defeated.

With the slave owner's codex dismantled, the invicta of the drum became the underlying rhythm. But what followed was a throttling international response. A trade embargo was invoked, creating for Haiti a healthless inhalation, a gasping, stunted social specification which resounds to this day. Divides along class and color lines have become ingrown, with the loss of living minimums continually provoking intolerable commotion.

Rife with inevitable corruption, with hunger, with taint by psychic deprival, suffering amongst the populace has almost become telepathic. Yet, with all the aforementioned negations there remains the spectacular contagion of a "New World voudou," the rage of ubiquitous Petro rites, where a skiagraphic sun continues to enliven a populace hounded by conspiratorial crippling, which from 1804 has continued to resound in the subtexts of edicts repetitively issued from the capitals of the West.

SINGING IN
MAGNETIC
HOOFBEAT

I can sit right here, think a thousand miles away.
—MEMPHIS JUG BAND, "Beale Street Mess Around"

The blues, like a drone of magnetic hoofbeats, insidious, miraculously hones as an incandescent Mustang artery. It is a wildness soaked in starvation and poverty, steeped in anomalous intensity, in tumultuous poetic contrast. A tradition brewed from an unsettled holocaust of ghosts. And these ghosts eternally linger in the voice as treacherous proof of the Middle Passage, with its bony antibouquets and sharks, with its pall of murder, with its lists inscribed on bloodstained wood. By even conservative estimate the Atlantic crossing claimed 100,000,000 African lives, a number which is seldom broached, even in the most enlightened of discussions. It takes on the specter of an inverse calendric, of a dark consternation and silence, which is dialectically opposed to the more acceptable celebrations of the American spirit, be it that of "Independence Day" or the unquestioned wintry salute to George Washington, praising his heraldic deeds during the contradictory days of the early republic.

But when treading upon this unmoving holocaust of blood, the typical reaction of denial is expressed. At best it is summoned from the mists as a negligible proto-history, as a strange but chimerical gerund never officially addressed within the annals of historicity. I am Black, and I speak Dutch or English, and I exist within the incessant confines of Paramaribo or Los Angeles, or I enunciate my existence in Spanish from an oblique hovel within the mysterious confines of Caracas, I merely reflect the language of my enslavers, who have distorted my African totality, my inscrutable matrix lamp, my natural Ashanti upheaval. By carrying these languages I do not express through them the conviction of a patriot, forever beholden to their Euro-historic objectives, artificially imposed upon my African reflex and world view. These languages merely exist as veneers, as a kind of transplanted wattage, mingled with centuries of bitterness; not one day having passed throughout the previous seven centuries without some Black person being subject to harassment or murder. The official chronicles dispense with this darkness, and instead seek to build around this experience superfluous emblems of exotica.

Given this background, we have never known peace, and have remained in perpetual soliloquy, balancing our psychic dice, waiting for the moment, for the power of our original coalescence, so as to reshape the void and transmute its rays, with the light of our universal animation. We are not immune to treachery, or to laws which maniacally condone our mistreatment. So when Europeans stare into our unmitigated cauldron, there is nothing but fire, nothing but broken lava trees, singing in misplaced vulture's emphatic. The diaspora remaining a perpetually angered field, threatening, untenable, flavored by the nectar of bondage. So, in every society in which we've found ourselves marooned, there has always been an altering of language, of custom, of culture, from their original base, as designed by the Euro-colonial. This being the case, there always exists the impending curse of eruption, of marking time around the sullen world of an erratic rattlesnake volcano. Of course, I have taken a generic bush and shaken it, so as to bestir eruptive leeches, so as to light up the coffers of ignition. And so, from this African brush-fire bush comes the blues.

Black Bottom McPhail, Elmore James, J.B. Lenoir. I bring forth these names from my upward earthquake sluices, from classic burn marks on the heart. I could just as easily speak of Texas Alexander, of Blind Lemon Jefferson, of Victoria Spivey. All of them pour forth from the current of anger, of ambivalence, or humorous irony with its scalding seaquake snows. Speaking from this context it could simply be said that washing powder boils, that the crescent moon had become an optically blond rhinoceros hide. When I imagine at this level I think of the limitless scope of the blues, with its frustration and travel, with its humor and drinking. Revolt is its bread, its exclusive respiration, its soil. From this evolves its sinews, its glinting explorational fiber. This being the mode of its disruptive English, its antimemorials, its slow motion lightning.

The blues transmutes us to a zone replete with frogs and pistols, replete with voluminous cravings and revenge. And the singer is lit by a fundamental cipher which burns within the fires of pure imaginal moons, where the lyric is momentarily poised upon a spider's talons, between eclipse and risk. And what transpires is the constant threat of incarceration and death. The time, the early 20th century. The place, the postplantation South, and the claustrophobia of apartheid. Because of the latter condition the victims were affected with a self-directed anger, which pitted Black against Black, with an elliptical and unforgiving fury. It was life under the auspices of separation, under the auspices of arbitrary execution. Witness the bleeding Bessie Smith, barred from life-saving treatment. Her death remains a universal symbol of the post-Confederate South, marked by its trade in living umbilical skulls.

So, to pursue the blues as poetic calling was to leap through the fire of veracity at its brightest. It was to defy a world so assiduously studied by the Nazis, in which to be Black was to be condemned and psycho-physically interred in an institutionally devalued racial genetic. It was a world encircled by mephitic absolutes. Existential constraint by color. So rather than being an escape, or a cleansed and tapered poultice, the blues defied, it eluded the sinister embodiment of death traps, like a tragically mottled sylph, rising from the ethers of a negative grenadine imprisonment. The blues then taking on the peril of a roaring fish, partially scorched in a darkened natron river, with the pain of the elliptic scattered into non-eclipsing forms, so that the nuance of the voice carried an inverse explosive, strangely seared by infernal poetics. In his "Eisenhower Blues," J. B. Lenoir "threatened the ruling class with theft and by implication with expropriation . . ."[1] He sings:

> You rich people listen, you better listen real deep,
> If we poor peoples get so hungry we gonna get some food to eat.

Or take Bessie Smith when she sings:

> I'm bound for Black Mountain, me and my razor and my gun.
> I'm going to shoot him if he stands still and cut him if he runs.

Even the path of crime becomes a glow by which the life force transmutes itself into an angular scope of beauty, and becomes a fully enlivened drone, empowered by the sting of a previously kindled damage.

The blues at its essence protracts the core of African expression which is anathema to those of diurnal consciousness whom its sounds harass, like exposed skin at odd moments brushed by a flare of passing molten and thorn. It is the message of an uprooted fang, vile, and imaginal with tempestuous conquest. Emblematic with pain, the blues burns like a flaming vampire scroll in the face of a stunted Saxon morality. I imagine in 1929, a copper whore, Afro-Asiatic as to skin tone, slipping across the chastity of the color line in her platinum creosote stockings, breaking down the Christian marriage bed with her invisible Ashanti motifs. Diamonds are then wrecked, and the rational soul surreptitiously invaded.

From lyric to lyric secrecy intensifies, concerning the regimen of making one's way in this life. Therefore secrecy goes hand in hand with suspicion. When Jazz Gillum sings, "Don't touch me with your broom, don't let my lamp get low," he is expressing the universal instinct "of a doubt, of a countercurrent at work within him, whose force might, at the moment of execution subtract form the force of his intentions." 2 Thus the power of magic and omens, of the concentrated fever which illumines the mind when hearing a "rooster crowing when the sun goes down." The lyric becomes the raw yet inscrutable oracle which speaks of forces which smolder, which ambulate far away from brightened double mirrors with their consciously reflected reason. The breath then concurs at the pitch of nebulosity, "where the mind ranges freely beyond the confines of reality," where "insight suddenly and unexpectedly presents itself," entrancing the soul like a riveting and eclectic mural, where incredible realias intrinsically transpire by means of a curious, but liberating power. The latter is what I call the wing of imaginal African antigravity which flies above the soil of the universal reflex tree. The psychoemotional pitch of the dawn, of eros, of travel, of crime. I think of the Willie Dixon lyric, the Muddy Waters expression, the intuitive biographic of Sleepy John Estes, diving into his "river of whisky."

The array of revolt simply staggers, as if a weaving Mustang in a dream, into stampedes of Appaloosa, threading a mosaic of instinct disrupting Apollonian trails of resistance, where the moral sanctions blur, transmuting to a purity of apparitional logic. The blues in this regard, taking on carnivorous heightening, a dense repetitive looping, coterminous with musically ingested splendor sung in seamless metrical lava. The sound as an enigmatic brush fire beacon, like a sun above volcanoes, shimmering on lagoons newly born from Sphinxian transparency and glaciers. Its ironical grounding, its tempestuous schisms. So, to survey the blues, to extract from its flows a psychiatric germ, would be to circumvent its aura, to test its properties in isolation.

The diurnal penury of minds such as T. S. Eliot, or Ezra Pound, can have no coexistence with the blues. Why Eliot would be absolutely petrified if confronted with the potency of Lightnin' Hopkins, as a carouser, as a perpetual aficionado of drink. Therefore, the dust, the despair, the dreadful organics, tend to repulse the empowered, much in the way D. H. Lawrence reacted with hysterical disgust to a recording of Bessie Smith. And this attitude follows to the American majority who feel the blues musician conducts existence in a semi-human enclave, and is granted the dialogical status of a scorpion or a shark. Incommunicable, ancient, dangerous, oblique. The music is thus subject to an emptied botanical witch hunt, given the status as a purely poisonous cipher. When Elmore James sings of a sun in a dream on a rainy night, he is expressing the fertile activity of dreaming, with its blurred borders, with its open ended resolutions. Such lyrics soar beyond the stony fiefdoms of capital and work, instead meandering throughout a force field, haunted by cryptic intaglios, by wayward cartouches, stumbling through explosive powder fields. Expelled roots, sums of evaporated comets! Such are the songs which reinhabit their Gods, which spiral into African intensity, therefore, never an ethos of painful cowering, or the whispers of negated status. No, never a turning back, never a lyric forgery by daylight.

Witness the intense scrupulosity of Blind Lemon Jefferson when he screams at Lightnin' Hopkins for not playing with the required preciseness, not realizing his accompanist was a beginner, and nascent with age. The latter elements becoming known Lemon was able to transmute his original anger and help the 8-year-old Hopkins along. However, his original reaction shows a highly evolved purity comparable to a Lorca, or Césaire, with his life fidelity aligned to an inward consuming poetic. One would find the same spirit in the developed Hopkins, in his early mentor Texas Alexander. Or one could speak of Memphis Minnie, or Victoria Spivey in this regard.

Therefore the blues singer is never prone, or apathetic, or dyslexic with indifference. Smokey Hogg exists within an imaginal range which should be generally acknowledged as is the case say, with Lautréamont, or Uccello. The forays into splendor, the ferment, the color, yellowed and dazzling as moonrise in Mississippi. The old Delta, with its rain drops and parching, with its monstrous and racist accruals, only fueled the anger, the eruptive miasma, of a song form imbued with explosion and linkage.

A NEW LIBERTY
OF EXPRESSION

1

A torrent of thoughts, quaking ciphers, oscillating subtrahends. Such were the credenda of this conference, providing its participants with the freedom to leap the stereotypic, far outstripping the myopia of the didactic, thereby bringing into view the expansional repertoire of Afro-American written expression. It was an ambiance where old dichotomies no longer existed as models.

I'm thinking of the dilemma faced by Melvin Tolson, circa 1965, his imagination deleted by antipoetic debate. One the one hand, the myopia of the Anglo poetic establishment, and on the other, the didactic stridulation of the burgeoning Black Arts movement. His poetic complexity obscured, his splendor momentarily eclipsed by pervasive ideology. Only now is his *Harlem Gallery* being witnessed from its organic root. But it is because of the Melvin Tolsons, the Jean Toomers, the Bob Kaufmans, that our conclave was able to ignite, and continue to create an ongoing criteria.

No longer does one have to be an imaginal pauper, beholden to a recusant glance, constantly tethered to writing on ubiquitous repression.

And when I say repression, I am thinking of Saxon institutional attack, and our having to look into its fangs with the plain spoken speech of the hour. No. I know there is more. I know that I can no longer be restrained by methods diametrical to interior liberty. Yet I know such repression is not to be denied, not to be seen as some anachronistic hamlet conveniently obscured by modernity. The continuous attack upon the Afro-American psyche remains a psycho-emotional constant, with us, always navigating threat, throughout different heights of toxic water. Yet because of this, our imagination always awash in elusive complexity.

An Afro-centric complexity not solely bound to the American South and its experience of uncultivated sullage. I am not bound to 1619, and the convocation of our collective conscription to American soil. Let me speak of the "first seven dynasties" of the Pharaoahs, of Kemet's predynastic fires sprung from south of the Sahara. Sprung from the "oldest nation on record . . . the Nubian nation Ta Seti."1 So when I use language I am thinking of its African applicability. Not the legacy of the aforementioned South, with its continuing psychic confinement, with its resolute heritage of repression.

2

As Césaire has pointed out, Surrealism sparked the African in him. And I can say much the same, in that it has liberated my animistic instinct, so that I am able with unlimited range to roam throughout my writing. Be it radiolarians, or ocelots, or dictators who have merged with dissolution, the whole of life burns for me, existing without border or confinement. The sun, the air, the fires forming, the waters swirling without let-up.

So when working with these primordial forces language becomes an organic weapon. A weapon which clears out old toxins, which annihilates the autocracy of imaginal restriction. Because of this I am no longer condemned to pouring out lines soaked with acceptable didactics.

One can speak of dazzling fuchsia, of luminous waters on the moons of Saturn, all the while knowing that the animistic principle pervades one's endeavors. The ardor of one's voice transmuting all explanation. And this praxis of liberty was vibrant throughout the whole morning of my panel, "Tell My Horse," led by Giovanni Singleton. The Loas rode us. We were able to speak with abandon. Myself, C. S. Giscombe, and Julie Patton, were given the opportunity to shift the human field with a new liberty of expression.

A RELENTLESS

METEORITICS

POIESIS, ALCHEMY, COSMOLOGY

SPIRIT AND PRACTICE

Being menaced by consciousness, the poet finds that the magnetic inscription of words on the page is only part of a continuum. One's every movement, one's every despair, is empowered by a wild illuminant rush which burns at the base of one's character. This is the praxis of spiritus, the praxis of breath, in the simultaneous realms of the diurnal and the oneiric. This constant awareness seems always empowered by a surreptitious sun emitting its power through the aural canals. And the raw material of life is always transmuted by these aural rays. And because of the fire at this sensitive level, one is continuously placed in temperamental combat against the quotidian carnivore, against its reflexive muscle of fact.

Because of such ongoing warfare one's initial survival builds to the power of a continuous trance, where one is able to inscribe the imaginal in alleyways or on bus benches.

I once spoke of transforming the hound-dog palace by the fact of the imaginative characteristical presence simply because true poetic force is rare, and because of that rarity is able to dazzle in an ambiance of rock plants, and arid Geiger counter motives.

It is an incendiary rum, a luminous spectral blaze, as though freshly risen from a lightning struck cellular forge. One's advantage being superior use of language, the basic currency of human cognition. So when language is transmuted to another law, to a more profound melodics, it cannot help but influence the surrounding confusion with a new and transformative vibration.

ALCHEMY AS POETIC KINDLING

... poetry has no other mission than to transmute history. And therefore the only true revolutionary poetry is apocalyptic poetry. —OCTAVIO PAZ

It exists as a cycadaceous spur, as ceaseless motion towards gold. Its fire is brewed in concentrated spirals reflected in the phonemes as genetic nettling water. Poetry being the language of concentration through destiny.

One commences the poetic quest with a thirst for illuminate language, as if one had been branded in the womb, with the anti-linear condensed in the image. And I am not speaking of an affected, self-appointed heroics, condoned by escapist grammar, but conviction, burning like a phantom mesmerism, always calling one home to the fruit of one's bones.

Conviction like an intuitive vulcanism does exist, like a singular body of sound. And this sound pre-exists the composition of intensive parables or poems. It pre-exists the maturation of multilineal ideals. It is a condition in the way that one reflexively exists. Whether it exists in the way one holds a cup, or the way one pursues a suicidal interest in stars or iguana. One breaks the pattern, one severs the quotidian mode. Like a torrential truth pouring out invisible vibrations, the community is altered to a ghost at hand. Not a ghost, mind you, in the despicable popular sense, but nevertheless a ghost, who feeds on transparencies from birth. These psychic regions exist, are born and become alert through the power of poetic nigredo. And when fully ripened they explode with a-sequential pyroclastic, leaping the lower boundaries, existing in an ignescently transmuted reality. One surmounts each imaginary crippling by means of an injudicious language. One expands the realm of speech, one takes in odors, takes in foliage, takes in contraband. One speaks in alchemical atonality, in constant mercurial voltage.

So the alchemical poets find themselves genetically ensconced in the aforementioned nigredo. The proto-fires, the pre-emotive hurtling of language, the tenacious image foci seedlings.

We know about viridian meadowlarks being forced from the voice, about operant pinnacles obscured by the deadly haze of analysis. So how to destroy the great arthritic claw, that great arthritic burden that engulfs the mind with sequential hazard? With the intensity of the image, alive with its maturation by anger, by exhaustive whirling and craving, like a vampire after blood, in the penultimate clockwork before dawn. This is what Philip Lamantia calls the "Red phase" of the "Great work," when the linguistic voltage shatters the flank of despotism, of the transfixed form which masquerades as rigor.

Alchemical language is a passage through stages; and if we could see the visage of Hölderlin quickly flickering on a visual reel, we would readily sense the alchemical shadings, not through the force of our optical appendage alone, but through our sense of interior weathers, moving back and forth through linguistic turbulences. Ultimately, an elevated life atop "eternal mountains." And Hölderlin sees this elevation as a struggle, as he posits the difference between "the warm life" within, and "the icy history of common day."

An imagination precluded against contamination, where one could imagine a slaughterhouse producing arisen angelics, or imagine a griffin atop boulders staring out into a magically crafted dawn of magenta.

In the alchemical poet images arise from a high state of risk, from advanced flotational scarlet. I am not speaking of a secondary utterance conditioned by rigid laryngeal suture, but a vital deafening electrics, filled with incalculable summas. And this power is conditioned by development, each stage of the inner expression linked with the outer peril through which one passes, seasoned by melancholia, and darkness. As the poet traverses the covert domains, we witness the outer ironics, the flaws, the disasters, the handcuffs, the boundaries. One day composing in a lion colored villa, on another, destitute, scrounging, choking on liters of spittle. The contradictions inherent in the chemistry of risk, cradling torment in one's singing feathers, so as to magically rise from densely riddled charcoal lagoons.

And it is in this rising that mesmerism becomes synecdoche and spillage, where the words take on a butane color, in constant orphic transmutation. The eel, the fiery hull, the red and glistening princess, become elaborate, and take on the sonar of Herons. Then one gives the words power to fly through the eye of the skull. The poem transfixes without modeling, entrances without deciphering. Therefore, the ambiguity thrills, and opens up the reader to constant illuminal spiraling throughout a duration of simultaneous transparencies. The image then becomes a crystalline manna, a sun exchanging its forces with water.

Like Shelley or Artaud, the alchemical poet, by magically ingesting demons, is able to enunciate prophetic enigmas, is able to take as riddle a fount, which pours forth tenacious wanderings from an essentially rebellious interior. A gust of eternity from the voice, not as mechanical paradigm, but as a beautiful holocaust of monsters. A "nocturnal wolf at high noon," "standing in fields of blood," "laying down its entire chromosian hand," its image, glowing from the leaps of an oven, carving with its knives an inconsolable mercury, so as to hew out the void, with an odor of "immaculate" frenzy.[1]

And if it is one thing the poet requires it is heat. It is the multiple and enduring friction which honors its lashing out and bewitchment. And from each quotidian annihilation comes a fruit of a higher and greater energy, of a fire of fertile and surreptitious turquoise. The poet in this era of the past 200 years has had to surmount the power of tyrants and magicians, and has had to take on the authority of a phantom egret ruling from a transparent throne of sound. Rimbaud and Campana can be deftly described in glossolalia and iguana, Artaud as fishing from a darkened deck of veins, with Pessoa flinging his findings into absinthe and hamlets. These poets have committed war against the rational, and are right in keeping with Borduas and his seminal statement on "Global Refusal," with its resistance to "public opinion," to "ridiculous justice," to "general disapproval." In the works of these men there is always a copious frying, a schema of splintered stratification and absurdity. And whether it be in situ, or on the open road, a restless anger always prevails. An exploded salt, a seasoned mercury. And this anger is a gift which springs from the angle of work—the dialectics of the study hall and the brothel. It is a work which swallows discredit and venom, which takes on opprobrium, weaving from its hollows magical bells and glass. Over the past two and one half centuries it is the itinerant who has possessed us, who has inscribed the language of ecstatic delirium. Conversely, it is the scribes, the official pamphleteers that we vilify, that we seek to re-inter in oblivion. So when Césaire demands a sincere and internal African wholeness he is rebuffed by communist ideology, and told to burn his own solutions, to stuff his crows' nests with candles counted by machine and bureaucracy. He disembarks, and walks away from the ramparts, knowing full well that the bastion is the glow from within.

When discussing this level of energy, words like maniacal, absolute, seem to balance themselves on equators of terror. One does not self-serve, or superficially deflect, the maze, and the contradictory tediums of the moment. When Paz resigns his ambassador's bureaucracy because of student "blood in the Plaza de los Sacrificios," he unloads himself of "bile," and takes on water, restoring a level of dignity.[2] He underlines defiance as honor, which throttles neurosis, which upends deception. Therefore the alchemical poet exists as a dangerous vagrant, chattering in elusive cobalt, walking in a personal zodiac garden, trailed by "Raw Sienna" moons glowing on the backs of Zebra.

And I'll always remember my first encounter with Bob Kaufman, at an angle on a street in North Beach, wordless in his phantom movements, like the silence of an alchemical crucible. The nutrients inside his skull like interior flashing muscles, his seismically arched back beneath fables of sonar. His lines, evolved from a beautiful alabaster tilting, from a blank zodiacal craving, continuing to send their signals with "secret Medici keys," with original "glacial" octave, farming grains with splinters from the sun.[3] Kaufman churns at the core of the alembic smuggling salts through his poetic ventricles. Seeing Kaufman in high relief, one can poetically graph "the symbolic meaning of the various alchemical operations," of "calcinations," of putrefaction, of "solution," of "distillation," which becomes "the coincidenta oppositorum," the union of "the male principle of consciousness, with the female principle of unconsciousness."[4] Images of a "face" . . . "like a living emotional relief map," or "the cry of amethyst heron," ascending from a magic germinal grave.[5]

This is poetry as "precipitate of pure time" (Paz), where the wheel stops, where fiestas boil. By its very nature poetry blinds us, and takes us levels and levels beyond abnegation. It thrives on linguistic rebellion, and is enemy of exchange and common monetary retrieval. The life of commerce it assassinates and purges, speaking with the force of irreducible intensity. In its essential register it is not clannish or ideological, it creates its own pattern with a relentless meteoritics. In the word, the phrase, exists the arch movement of language; and in this arch movement there exists the poetic flower speaking in clairaudient ramblings of chance. In this feverish metropolis of energy, there exist the sweltering electrodes of image, line, poem, breaking onto a fertile glycerin shore, where totems of fire stare amidst solvents of glass, into the motionless interaction of eternity. This is the realia of linguistic nobility, the height from which all cerulean evolves.

One could say that the poem is like a bird drifting off from a lightning tower of language, gliding through the miraculous circulation of infinity. A language of power which overcomes opinion and seasonal reaction. The best plays of 1944, the infected spinning of a popular romance chronicle. Instead, the poem is in league with a more enduring passion, not inclined towards rewards, or immediate outcome. As Garcia Lorca attests "I know he that is wrong who shouts "Now! Now! Right now!" with his eyes fixed" on immediate recompense and profit.

We live in a land where the popular expression has been imprisoned and engineered for the use of illusion and debasement. It is the mental equivalent of physical cholesterol and poison. And this is how the masses consume their weight in readily available cultural fat. The attention span stiffens, the absorption rate contracts, to a few feeble jabs of the memory. Any relatedness to deeper strata of feeling is annulled, and if allowed to momentarily surface, is insidiously tainted with a pejorative metaphysics. Therefore a more refined perception takes on the status of debility, of an ably endowed fraud, or a weirdly empowered anemia. With the commercial tenet at hand the artist loses the mark of maturation, and the poetic combat with the invisible. How can the commonly hailed image cope with suffering and transmutation? How can it seethe with the letters of the dream? As rejoinder there is spareness, a sculpting according to fickle tastes and momentary tenets. Nothing but straw, turned into a false and tufted cashmere. An impaired and ungracious linguistic capacity.

On the other hand in Bali, when the witch-queen Rangda appears, the visible and the invisible instantaneously exist. Rangda, with her "curved white fangs," with "her yard-long . . . tongue," with her "goat hair wig," carries power from the visible to the invisible, returning again to affect the visible. This of course reflects a society with refined psychic circulation. A sensitive astral theater. This is the point where Artaud lost his public in the West. He sought a thrilling catharsis of existence for both performer and audience as one unbroken flow. He desired an inhabited theater, an impalpable poetic theater. Instead, what he confronted was theater as a fort for legal entertainment, to be forgotten upon entering the boulevard. What Artaud called for was a poetics of thirst, a striving for greater existence.

And we see this same carnivorous thirst in another country, in an earlier time, when Lopez Velarde enters Mexico City, discovering his language through doubt, who like Artaud was able to chart his anguish, always challenging the drama of parochial assumption. In "The Malefic Return" or in "Ants," or in "I Honour You In Dread," there is the bitten inch of the nail, or the percolation of wine in a coffin. Like Artaud his writings take on an alchemical bravado, speaking with previous imponderables. Not a poetry of duplication, or a sum of emotional forgeries, Lopez Velarde has stated that he longed "to eject every syllable that is not born of the combustion of my bones."[6]

Therefore poetry seems fed by aggravation and danger, by opprobrium and fatigue, like a current pulsing through ignescent waters. Bewilderment and perfection by bewilderment. Superficially ambiguous yes, but in terms of its deeper archery, poetry is able to open its target congealed in lightning. It carries the power to illumine, to exemplify transformative purity and stamina, which predates Homer, which survives the blast of Armageddon.

EXACTITUDE

Not didactic addition, or superimposed forensics hoisted upon a psychic limestone slab, but exactitude, as a state, over and above the blizzard of static. A static made up of integers, and forms of integers, empowered across its field by exoteric procreation.

Fact at the level of popular cerebral exhibit, can never organically respirate as poetic neural balance. The latter experiences itself as auric exploration, which inevitably accrues from auric harmonics. Again, right balance. So sums at this level are akin to Daumal's savor, where essences intermingle, where the facts of the world then partake of the zone of tintinnabulation.

POETRY

ALCHEMICAL ANGUISH AND FIRE

Two Interests: the core of reality in
the one case, language in the other—...
is the double concern of poetry.
—YVES BONNEFOY ON RIMBAUD

Poetry commences by the force of biographical intensity, by the force of its interior brews, by the sum of its subconscious oscillations.

It is like a nettling piranha spurring the voice with condensed alchemical pain. It is the voice which elusively rises above the perils of "debased existence," as a realia of flashes, as a realia of soaring lightning ramifications. At this level of transparency, the breath takes on movement, so that phonemes, and words, and phrases, fuse in the superior blood of an incandescent Bengal splendor.

Within this irruption of the igniferous, words are capable of universal poetics; and I mean by universal, possessing the power of pyretic plasticity. In consequence, the language of botany, or medicine, or law, takes on a transmogrified dictation, where their particulars blend into a higher poetic service, in which they cease to know themselves as they were, thereby embarking upon a startling, unprecedented existence.

In the midst of such concentration, if I name "the constellation Do-rado," it is not the same Dorado of the astronomers, nor does it carry the same set of values when placed within a page of rigorously balanced astrobiology. It is a new Dorado, capable at one touch of expansion and Utopia. It automatically becomes an enemy of the quotidian, an enemy of fixation and separation. It burns, it takes up the incandescence which the civil systems shun. It becomes a rich imaginal shadow flowing through a verbal lens of miracles. Then there is no longer the dried eradicated stanchion of word as use, of word as measuring rod, of word as rational entrapment. The voice then ceases to conclude on a point, or stare at surrounding virtues for approval. It is inevitable, so therefore the separations, the isolations, the blank tumescent counting patterns are exploded, much the way contracted stars erupt, giving off new, portentous living material for forms of further expansion.

Poetics which reduce, which didactically inform, take on the infected measures of the gulag. During the earlier part of the 1950's we see the poet Césaire in sustained resistance against this gulag. He takes on the Communist Party boss Aragon and his demand for plain spoken diacritics, for abject poverty of description. Instead, Césaire places foremost the unfigurable party, who like Lautréamont leaves no traces, leaves no plaintive dots across the wrecked biography of literary law. And it is from this latter example that I gain a powerful internal momentum in using a language in natural combat against ideology, against the popular phrase symbiotic with common herding technique and sterility.

So for me to erect memorials, to take up with my pen neo-Freudian resurrections, or to give in to false antiblasphemous façades, would be to color myself wretched, locked in a penultimate forgery of the fetid. Of course the scholars would appraise me with their niggling sort of glimpses, they would examine my footnotes, and even in their minuses give me credit for a poetic action or two. But this is not life. This is not the fiery, the musically sumptuous cross-hatching, where the invisible burns, where the angels flare up and exfoliate like magic.

There is the ceaselessness, the arcane of ruses, the multiple tonics compressed in an image. From this arises a life of boundless thirst, a life which honors and amalgamates the velvet of the "Imago Ignota," the "obscure," the harmonious "remoteness," taking one on a voyage beyond the clarity of an imprisoning foci of lenses.

Enough with finance, enough with the hunt for allegorical tumors. Poetry explodes the hexahedron, vertically connecting the higher and lower spheres, by the plentiful frictions of anguish and fire.

TRANSGRESSION
OF GENRE
AS VITALITY

Transgression as fire, as magic generating agent, which eats at the axial monolith of genre with fumes from an encroaching lava. A feral lava of transmuted sting rays, of philosophical assault tribes, become a hurricane of verbal androgyny.

Who best mines such auricular aspect?

Lautréamont, with his exquisite fervor and menace, the penultimate Artaud, with his fury by x-ray and scalpel, Breton, with his furtive and occulted *Nadja*, and Césaire, with his devastating grace, with his explosive cross-hatching. In the works of these beings the blunted claws, of say, a Racine or a Trollope, have been attacked and mesmerically dissected with the power of a magnetic cutting diamond. Within the aura of such transfigured works one gets the feeling of watching a sturgeon, both solferino and xanthic, alchemically break across the confines of a smouldering sodium lake, empowered by the nutrients of poetic aural seed.

Works, not recast for groping in a universal graveyard, but works which shatter the model of "external arrangement." Vitality as insidious ferment, creating images which burn like a series of tubercular pole stars shifting through sudden realias of salt. A new sociology of wandering, of personality cast adrift, recasting their dice from forms of mysterious sullage.

After 500 years, the Renaissance has squandered its final yields of mercury, with its description of a nascent and re-arisen Europa, vanished, with the latter's 3,000 years of reasoning utterly sundered by its monomial use of classification. And from the collapse of this seasoned rigidity commences a flow of innumerable Nadjas, of splendiferous anti-heroines, suffused with a blank myopia which strengthens. Therefore, the old construct of text, with its tense compartings, into "epic, lyric, and dramatic," no longer inspires duration, no longer keeps us crucially riveted across the random field of living. The daily news reflects the prophetic anticipations of *Maldoror*, the African ferment of Césaire, like a birth of unspeakable multitudes condensed in world wide indigenous transition, away from the model of Europe with its condoned imperial butchery of outcasts. Transition occurs, and the once immaculately beheaded, now stand up like a mirage of linguistic androgynes.

Webster's describes genre as "a kind; sort; type." Classification which limits, which parallels surcease. I think of a flock of kings with edicts, written in a language adhering to a strict formation of boundary, to a form which claims as its power a recognizable constant. It is a feeling of fatigued Novembers, of heavy and moon burdened sunsets, embodied in "rhetorical mechanism," which condemns the flow of utterance to a strictly regulated decorum. Genre as exterior garment empowered by a counted archaeology of ghosts.

Two questions need always be asked: does the form contain life? Does it naturally abound with affective irradiation?

I would answer them this way: written creation is like an illusive flood of grams which mesmerizes in any form which sustains it. Because Homer wrote in metrics in no way condemns his epic intuition. On the other hand, pedantic incursion into the surreal stultifies, takes on the character of frozen disadvantage, as a rock-like ensemble of image. So what accrues from the latter is an unvarying sun, or a sea eternally shaped like a fossil.

For me, creation always probes, is a kinetic diorama, is a movement of encounter with forces. It is a mixture of peculiarity and mystery, which is a thirst that documents the sufferings and the powers as he or she has been moved to present them. Therefore we find immobility as a curse, as an ironical velocity of darkness. Yes, velocity as negative, as bound by despicable containment. In this sense genre deforms creation, and becomes a body of reasoned dictation, which freezes the leap, which frustrates emotions of chance. So for the magnetic creator power is never a poultice or a dying glycerin food, but the compound promiscuity of the adder welling up from within. Of course, it is the necessitous domain of fire, it is the dictated sun spewing out a galaxy of voltage.

Such voltage illumines the claustrophobic summa of *Maldoror*. Lautréamont, invested with the nobility of a Uruguayan vulture, began devouring the genres of their flesh and their blood, so that they definitively fell at the end of the 1860's, leaving the reader to wander through the thickets of immense albino grail, immersed in a strange expanding comprehension. "The work of Lautréamont shatters" the literary "expectation."[1] Historical "personality" is expunged, the biography expelled into the outer districts of conundrum, plunging the critic into the ruthless explosives of the text. Because what Lautréamont does with the power of his faceless glare is to destroy the burdensome notoriety of the author. His images cannot be subjected to a predecessor's marquee of anecdotes, to elements culled from arthritic chronologies. He thereby escapes the censor of the orthodox. "*Maldoror* . . . with its bewildering and deliberate multiplicity of literary registers" dispels for the conventional reader the reeking lineage of assumption. There is no taking into account the latter's limitations. On the contrary, Lautréamont attacks these limitations sparing nothing that would approve of a savageless conduct ambulate behind the bones of bureaucratically dulled literary barriers. Within the cyclone of *Maldoror*, Lautréamont creates "a little novel of thirty pages," the writing itself an exercise in "reductio ad absurdum," making it impossible to revert to "the manner of Flaubert, and Balzac, and Dickens." In this ironical menagerie he utterly destroys the dominating stereotypes,of "the dreamy adolescent," and "the retired naval commander" with "his timid, ladylike wife."

This being the atmospheric sodium which some 80 years later captivates Artaud, and inundates his glossary with explosives. An oeuvre of inscrutable praxis, in which drawings fuse with the gestures of the stage, impassioned radio chronicles electric like his motions in front of the camera, with the critical writings, the letters, the edicts, all writhing up the high road of the poetic. Artaud's odyssey calls to mind the serpentine lines as they move through Masson's drawing entitled "Furious Suns." A simultaneous field with the single form transcended. This is the human state in the high realms of the arcane, at its most multiple and eclectic, within the chromosomal flames of spontaneous dialectics. No exterior instruction is given as to the way energy of living condenses. Unclassifiable, magnetic, it was his runic and blistering desire which drove him to make the absonant connections between Van Gogh, Heliogabalus, and Dreyer, between the distant locales of Mexico and Ireland. The stasis of genre becomes a darting pen on a page, at a level of permanent meandering.

So when Nadja appears within the mirror of her ungraspable habitat, Paris dissolves in the writing of a charged cortical liquid. A being who burns above "banality," who scoffs at adoration and simplicity. Her presence, a sheaf of electrodes, tossed by the pitch of psychic inner wind. Her conduct could easily be described as a sea of scorpions, or a disconcerting parable. Yet one thing remains certain, Nadja acts as a cure against the power of mechanical synopsis. She brings to rational content an anti-declaration, a movement of oblique ciphers across a haunted boulevard of water. An altered physicality persists as Nadja precipitates objective hazard, her intangible mortality like a floating perception of signs destroys by its very nature narrative relation and the latter's connective to structure by means of gullible motif. For Breton, the describing of Nadja as novel amounted to no more than the intolerable acid of insult, genre being nothing more to him than the decadence of a bygone foliage, or anthem.

As further corroboration, 13 years after his Nadja, Breton appears in Martinique, and meets Césaire, and brings him to objective refulgence. Like Nadja, Césaire is illusive and wayward, but in a more explosive register. He poetically slashes, he inveigles his body, while sniping at the shards of Vichy. He is the intermittent clarion who, in work such as his Cahier, or in his "Les Armes Miraculeuses," dazzles as an anti-existence escaping containment into the utter enigma of reality. No literary habit or outline takes form in these texts. They are free, and magically live like a torrential flash of honor rendering light to his war torn readers, guiding them to new provinces of passion. Cleansed, by the obscure power of the unpredictable, he supersedes chronology making it shed its heavy ice in a vacuum. Therefore, the rational can no longer render itself to itself, and collapses like a body into a vat of ennui. Such writing collects by its motion spectral intensity, ascribing to itself the electricity of the occult. Genre, being weighed in such context becomes an evanescent portion, with its previous parameters now the equal of an acknowledged nonsubsistence.

The energy once contained behind the barricade of prose, or soldered within the coffin of poetry, is now free and beautifically transmutes into a poetic galaxy of sanguineous stellar rotations. No longer author with axial identity, no longer creations successfully baited by academic forces of repression. Across the prairie of the page there can be botany, cataclysms, nightfall, simultaneously expressed in single lines, and dense multilayered sentences. The amperage of mixture, of surreptitious masquerade, wandering like a skittish horse across moats of sparkling iridium, leading to a hall where a greenish turpentine angel is addressing in occulted Farsi an antimimetic gallery of skulls. A vitality in its rendering, yes, but not in terms of narrative accumulation, but as vigorous insurrectional sonar, empowering its hermetic enclave with spirals of whispering salt, magically floating beyond the graves of a pungent creosote compound.

THE BIRTHMARK

A CROP OF DARKENED CITRON
FLOWERS EXPLODING IN THE SKIN

It is a strange moment
of this landscape of this whole world
that seems to go beyond its own existence
—PHILIP LAMANTIA, "A Winter Day"

A sign, a mark which looms from prephysical explosion. Yes, the mark which exists and retains its relentless glaring beyond the black siroccos of the kindled sorcery we call death. The mark of the human voyager who has magically emerged from seeming disadvantage, as if singed by impalpable confusion, by subversive concordance, spawned in the wake of a mysterious invalid's nostrum. The birthmark always the glimpse of the powers of predestiny, of the "three-brained" being sired by illegible forces. Illegible, not in the sense of ignited falsification, or of transdissected dread rationally contained within armor, but akin to a runic zone from which meteors and blazing shrapnel emerge. Therefore, the birthmark implies that the body is not simply the mortar of a random quotidian pamphlet. It implies interior continuity, it implies the restless mysteriums in human living exposure. And by living I am concerned with those primordial signals etched like transdimensional lithoids which empty and transpire at the cusp of parturition.

Think of the birthmark as the remains from a kinematic holocaust, as sphinxian reticularity, as velocity embedded in sudden hurricane locality.

Within the arc of the blemish there is the harmonious whole, whose fascination exists in its remoteness, in the "unknown," in "the antecedents and the aftermath" of the beautific as human identity. That which surrounds the human body, that which the intelligence is "incapable of apprehending, or appropriating" within the skulled five senses.

If one could psychically open a pigment, or magically explore its contents, neither would one find a ludicrous animosity, or imploded mortuary steps, but the fascinating shores of mirage-like, reddish hemangiomas. Not as the clinicians describe explosive blood vessel growth at the surface of the skin, but as anomalous invictas literally burning with mystery, like a beauty inspired by regressive volcanoes.

And here the gulf expands beyond prenatal detection. The "chorionic vilii sampling," or the drawing of fluid during the fourth month of pregnancy, called by the medic Amniocentesis. Saying such I am casting the birthmark into the zone of a primeval centigrade, into monodic Calliopes which illumine an asymptotic frenzy, floating in the uterus as a signature of riddles.

Because to witness a vertical mark the length of the forearm, or espy other black and reddish samplings strewn across the waters of the skin, I am compelled to embrace the fertility of conundrums, with their a-conceptual roulette scattered across the species. In this way I am like that hermetically marked Egyptian who sees in the diamond of the moon the "Ibis religiosa," who runically strides across a cubit of fish, who marks the occult heart with the beauty of irregular beating. This being such, the body emblazons its zone as a "terrestrial maze," as a hypnotic integer, as a hypostatic firmament, capable of gliding beyond any awkward ambulation. Bodies for me consist of a spherical erubescence, of fabulous incarnadine foliage metamorphically concealed in dark hereditary meadows, amidst colossal indigo hieroglyphics, pavonine, archaic with inner caliginous cascades.

This to me, the true study of sulphur and its habits, its mixture of scrutiny and divination by number. Therefore, its motion of glare and darkness being its true Egyptian conjuration, suddenly able to plummet like birds from the superficial to the profound. It understands the "lower waters" of "protomatter," and its essential dialectic of angelic fissure, the latter assuming vertical spurts of lakes in formation.

It is by such function that the birthmark appears, like a prefatalic anagram, like an aesthetic, yet alchemical truth, much like an old prophetic raven uttering at sunrise. This allows me to witness fabulous mixtures of glass glowing between weather and birds. Yes, a runic wind in the heavens reflecting an inscrutable delta of diamonds brewing inside a heavenly pylon of crops. The skin at this level becomes a natural imago irradiating ringlets, as in the scent of flying harrier fumes, as was the judgment of ancient eyesight, when the focus was tested as to its power to comprehend "Alcor the faint companion . . . of Mizar" one of the "seven stars that form the Big Dipper . . ." I am speaking here of power, of an intense cerulean keenness, nonaligned to a lost personal blinding, to a harried perceptual mephitics, quickly frozen and staunched before evolving the powers of living.

Intrinsically, the birthmark represents the brink between parturition and invisibility. The perplexity which continues to feed the monarchs' wells, the piacular lightning peninsulas, as if listening to grasses burn like signals passed between the storms of angelic uterine bodies. What follows are behaviors of elliptical salt, of astonishing gifts restored by self-infected endurance. Because each mark on the body claims its existence as a sigil, as a conundrum of some former holding water, as if a particular bovine at birth coincided with a stately wine of melodious spillage. A remnant, a prior form invested with equational udders, with a geometry of stains concomitant with darker interstellar specifics. As if each mark or stain had an aggressive but blinded outward scroll, while on the inside of its struggles, its angels began weaving eclipse wings from the light in sparkling demon's hides. So in the mark one can see the chaos, the dialectic, the ravaging, the indecipherable.

Witness the song of a tyrannical hummingbird, which appears and disappears, understood solely by the sun-enriched savant as random oracular transmission. Its random density being a mark, like a luminous nigrescence, on the side of the arm, on the inside of the face, or a sudden discoloration near the front of the loins, or near the base of the foot, aligned with momentous darker seasons, conjoined with recticular storms within the zone of the body. A mark can condense in the ambulatory gold of Lorca's implicit limp, or transmogrify its nature in the existential praxis of Kaufman's refusal to speak. So if the cells chaotically wander from the double poles of the body, the impetuous becomes heraldic, like an erratic social carrier of bees, or of secondary emblems, or of a bloodless bison aggregation.

Poetic inclination allows the clandestinely sighted to peer at magnetic Luciferians fabulously ensconced at The Hotel Armada, musically neutered by a missing frankincense deluge. Such neutering should not urge the beholder at every sleep-induced séance, to shatter the optical powers detached from an "onslaught of fiends." But to boil rice, to eat a fabricated castor sauce, to see the only veins of sacrilege as mandrake infusion. But this is the realm of mediaeval Christian spying songs, concerned that the "mark of a witch was a red or blue spot" on the field of the body, produced by some preinflicted abscess road. Tertullian's condemnation was against the Devil's mark, and agreed with the subsequent witch killers that the mark "will not bleed," that the oceans will give blood before the pricked mark will bleed. According to such belief, the condemned would be revealed by the prevalence of laconic wizardry, of the burdensome gathering of herbs by stealth, of concocting dastardly brews by means of clepsydras' static, of hurling through the dream of a sleeper, a stone of exploded needles.

On the back of my right triceps there exists a small caliginous desert in which swans pontificate and swarm who commune with intangible Lynxes as to the dreaded cascades of irruptive citron flowers. I can only hope, that because of this mingling, my thunders will remain unchecked, that my eyes will begin to glow like a thousand thrust blades, exchanged like the menacing stealth projected between lions and hyaena.

So fatality, like an emptied disregard of simple collaboration by stricture, inscribes my obsidian leper's robe with the transparent power of a king, with a dark habitual scarlet in one hand, and with the power of the other casting dice in my syllabics, thereby allowing the compost to rave in an empty palingenesis, where the galaxies are distilled, and given over to a Lydian and rhapsodic Elysium annularity.

PRONOUNCEMENT

The veracity of drawing remains for me, the alacrity, power, and depth of line, welling up form the meteoritic human interior, always possessed of a magical fervor. Its smoldering destiny rivets the hand during composition, so that the images swiftly take on density and shape. By the very richness of its expressive force line implies by its very motion an array of colors temporarily occulted by the intensity of the graphite. Then the transfer of the drawing to a larger field of color becomes a very natural, organic evolution.

Being primarily a poet, visual expression is like stepping into the waters of a parallel music. Its perpetual novelty gives me a leonine momentum, allowing me to explore the imagistic depths with poetic "inner trembling." The compositional result continues to pour forth beings, part plant, part human, part celestial, always resonant with the original Silurian spark of creation.

GREEN

It absorbs and engenders empyreans. It is the color anterior to suns, being the source which seeds eruptions on Io. It is the color I associate with interior transpicuity, with vernal interiority. Its color is one with "the centre . . . of being," with its blue and yellow haloes emitted from its presence as subsequent respiration. I call it "the Great Work," the miraculous inception, the simultaneous engenderment.

There exists about it a shimmering philosophical prosperity, a Trinitarian blue sea which expands beyond the scope of numberless arcana, as transrational scintillation, as impeccable areola, understood within the human view as luminescent Monad, as "perfect form," as container of all substance.

Green in this regard, as the impalpable fire source, as scatheless complexity, which appears and transpires and returns to itself as totalic intimation.

A POETICS OF
THE IMPALPABLE

Each lingual seed, from the phoneme, to the fully osculate image, empowered the hypnotic rays of an inward vertical sun. Language, drawn towards its light, jets upward like an imaginal army of molten, of green inscrutable hieroglyphs charged with a magical insouciance, partaking not only of subconscious lunation, but also of the surreal hypnotics of the wonders of terra firma, its perpendicular momentum alchemically merging with the supraconscious realms where the spiritual sun empowers the impalpable.

So always there exists for me language as incandescence, as power which brews as magnetic food, capable of sustained hieratic foliage, where the upper and lower realms converse in aural bursts of transformative cinder, leaving the old partitioned capillaries behind. And I'm speaking not just of the subconscious force and its envelopment of daily reality, but also of the demonic and angelic lavas, with their magical poles, like the iridescent flight of a vampire, analogous to verbal fuel, which fuses the poet with the aural zone, of a totemic, transformative realia.

TAKING ISSUE WITH UBIQUITOUS REDUCTION

To be forbidden one's volcanisms, one's quarrels, in favor of the dust of a plainspoken warren, is to exist in terms of ubiquitous reduction. Language in its purest state exists as primal capacity, and the challenge of such capacity is to engulf delimitation, to advance the circumstance which completely alters the common mean. And by the common mean, motion is understood as digressive utterance, always in keeping with quarterly reports, with scheduled breaks, with logs which replicate pre-planned proceedings. To such perspective I remain extreme, being no more to the civil eye than a cave fish, or a cephalopod, or the strangeness of an owl combined within the remnants of an ice bear. I utter sound, but it is not prone to the same template as the work bench, as the written thoughts from the paymaster's dungeon. I say this because as poet I owe my utterance to other saturations, to other exhibits of sonority. As if I were a hawk shunted aside, as if my singular utterance sprung from indigenous Malay. Perhaps my English is the parallel of indigenous lorikeet or Malay. Perhaps it is a network of glass scattered by sonorous visibility, where the Sun proclaims a different hue, where the dawn rises backwards, where the sea enacts its weather from a parallel momentum other than the moon.

VENTRILOQUAL LABOR

As species after species implodes through disappearance, it seems the most propitious moment to commence upon a most scorching labor, a seeming nebulous labor, teeming with vibrational obscurity. I'm speaking of biokinetic elevation, so as to initiate communion with conscious collectives in the heavens. Not odyssey by machine or reason, but odyssey by soma, being nothing other than alchemical threading, connected to the larger galactic intelligences.

We face an insidious planetary future, collectively depleted by random cold, and patternless heat. The future, and the immediate future is like watching humanity being squandered inside a graph of poisoned condor's milk. It's as if an inward pole were shifting, leaving the living collective dulled by a withered orientation.

We are now left with inhuman probes, attempting to distill the outer worlds, yet compromised by their sporadic mechanical dysfunction. The nature of cosmic space being of such bizarre and invincible distance can never be apprehended by mechanical inquisition, never giving us the evolved level of communion which the race has subconsciously yearned for. So we are left with cellular objects, with electronic mails, with chatting rooms condensed by computer.

In this sense, the earth is proto-desolate, not so far as one would think from the primal desolation that one finds, while viewing vistas like Phobos or Ceres. In fact, in my present imaginal eye, I see nothing but skittish biblical tribes, modern, ghastly, flamelessly traversing speculation with vocables of blurred leakage. Codes, verbal strychnine clauses, each movement of thought being strategy as disaffection.

What I prefer to sense, is a honing by human alchemic, to a zone where ventriloqual hearing would transpire. And by ventriloqual I am thinking of a rhythmical glottic, defining a "resonant pathway," "a cosmic lifeline" extending "from the solar plexus through the reflective membrane of the planetary field on to the sun, and ultimately to the galactic core." The "road to the sky," "the invisible galactic life threads," which resonates the human soma with the "Planetary Circuit," with the "Solar Circuit," with the "Galactic Circuit."[1] An instantaneous hierology.

But in the lower gulfs, the mind is condensed by stultification and rancid plumage. Abstract methodologies are applied to the "galactic sea." A realia, totally conceptual in demeanor. A province of being only partial as concerns human bioelectrical possibility. Ultimately, a prosaic rendering of experience. In contradistinction, there is poetic inclusion of the cosmic electrical field. As poets, as imaginal intuitives, we have reached the realm of darkened centigrade plantings, where we implode by aural glimpses the upper intangibles of language. The slippages, the transparencies, the ventriloqual anopsias, further tuning the sonic register, thereby giving rise from the human soma to an intangible explorational geometry.

Under the mores with which we presently cope, this is the labor of an occult brethren, singing their sigils from an obscurity, scattered, haunted, irregular with dazzling. For instance, I breathe in one zone of the earth, always subject to waking transmutation. Another of us transmits this euphoria while traveling in Switzerland. Another of us feels blackly propelled through the powers of sleep. This is not unlike the initiatory work of the Buryat shaman in Siberia. Though physically scattered, we combine in this effort by means of ahistoric telepathy. Action then combines like a manifesto of ghosts, spinning their inclement gems like rays across various boundaries. Be they across earth, or seeing certain planets, in the zone around Alpha Centauri.

Each utterance from this state is praxis by interior accuracy. As in traditional societies it combines with energies which brought the Sun to existence. This being the removal of abstraction from energy, the erasure of parsecs from being. It is spontaneous connection to the cosmos.

So when Miró lights up a canvas with blueness, when the utterance of Lorca is totally subsumed in neurological transcendence, what I say is not without precedence in the recently living past. There are whole lists to be drawn from. But this is not the range for that kind of argument. I am concerned with language which breathes through explorational magnetics, alchemically superseding the poisonous metrical weight of our era.

THE ZONE
ABOVE HUNGER

Since the rise of the warrior city-states the controlling bureaucracies have exerted a trenchant power on the populations within their purview. An artificially divided strata arose from this world view, and a demand for menial labor became paramount. Under such auspices a select few were automatically absolved of the ulterior puzzle of day to day sustainment. But for the vast majority the issue of hunger and general dearth has maintained itself as the mantra of a negative epic. And it is within this epic that the majority of the populace in the West has been born.

From the 1760's onward a working class has evolved from the industrial epoch which was engendered at that time. A class, worked to its teeth in order to maintain a modicum of raiment and shelter. And it is this latter condition into which I was born, always near the margins, at times, only an eyelash from penury.

But as an artist, a poet, one does not have to curtail one's power in order to evoke the suffering which comes from material deficiency. Inner radiance cannot be curtailed by the stones one has to sup with one's bread. One can look at Rimbaud or Blake, at Césaire or Bob Kaufman, to see that the mind cannot be contained within the provinces of hunger.

And this is not to say that the reality of poverty has no life in letters, or that the imagination is elitist. By no means. But what I speak of is the imaginal power to leap beyond the brutally imposed confines to combat the bureaucracies with an elemental seismics, with a new and alien thinking.

THE WAY ONE SPEAKS,
THE WAY ONE WALKS

INTERVIEWS AND A LECTURE

HAULING UP GOLD FROM THE ABYSS

AN INTERVIEW WITH WILL ALEXANDER

Conducted by Harryette Mullen in
Los Angeles on November 29, 1997

HARRYETTE MULLEN: Will, I'd like to begin by getting some basic biographical information, such as when and where you were born, where you grew up. Who were your parents? How do you think your family and community might have influenced you in your early years? Your book, *The Stratospheric Canticles*, is dedicated to your parents, Birdie and Will Alexander. How did you come to be interested in books and writing?

WILL ALEXANDER: I was born in Los Angeles, and what's interesting for me is that Black writers of Afro-American persuasion are so often touted as being either Southerners or Harlemites, and I'm neither. I'm an absolute Westerner.

HM: Did your folks come from the South though?

WA: They did, but they have been here for so long that they had—

H M: They're Angelenos?

W A: Yes. There were actually Angelenos.

H M: But where did they come from?

W A: My dad was born in New Orleans. My mom was born in a small town in Texas. Marshall, Texas. I myself went to the South as a child once, and that was it. I never really had much contact, although my uncle's been quite an activist in politics back there, and has been for many, many years. In fact he's still active. He's part of—he's in the State Legislature. [The two elder Alexanders, Will and Avery, have passed away since this interview was conducted.]

H M: What's his name?

W A: Avery Alexander. He was a boxer as a younger man and led some very powerful rallies that helped to defeat David Duke. He led large rallies against David Duke and he has national stature as a labor leader, a labor organizer. So the family—in fact I brought an essay I wrote on my dad that just got published [*Apex of the M*, issue 6; also inlcuded in this volume]—the family started buying property and land in 1897, and they were not hesitant about keeping the white people off their land. I was told that my great-great grandfather would keep his pistol out [to warn racist intruders]: "Get off my property or I'll shoot you." So it's basically a very, very independent family on my dad's side, and my mother was even independent of her own very independent family. She transcended the independence of her family. She worked very hard, and she had magic in her. She was able to work with her intuition, and it was astoundingly accurate. She would say something, and it actually would happen.

H M: She was clairvoyant?

W A: She was clairvoyant, absolutely. So I would say that's where my poetry connects with clairvoyance, and from my dad I think I get a long-term stability.

HM: Do you know when they came out here and why?

WA: It was during the time of, as they say, the Second Great War, a war that also liberated Black people from the South, because the racially segregated South as everybody well knows was an inspiration for Hitler's Germany. I've always had a bad feeling about the whole area. My family felt the same way. They wanted to get out of their situation, so they met up and somehow forged a life here on the West Coast, like so many who migrated during the time of the war to places like Chicago, Philadelphia, and Los Angeles.

HM: Was your father in the war?

WA: Yes, he was. He was a sailor. His ship was hit by a bomb, but it didn't sink. They were lucky. I mean, it blunted the ship but didn't actually hit, out in the Pacific. He'd been to Japan and to the Pacific Islands, and also to Jamaica. He was interested in the situation of seeing Black people in power, doing things, whereas, when he comes back to the States, it's just the opposite. So his views were very independent, and I grew up looking at life with this double focus. The clairvoyance and this ability to hold my balance. I never fit in with the regular people, and I was never involved with any gangs either. Growing up in South Central was interesting because it's an all Black community. Overall it wasn't a bourgeois community . . .

HM: What kind of work did your parents do?

WA: My mom never worked outside the home, and my dad worked for the Department of Water and Power.

HM: That's steady.

WA: Yes, he was very steady, incredibly steady. I just saw him a little while ago. He has some problems now, but he's getting better. My mom passed away a few years ago. They were both really independent people, and that created an independent streak in me. I was never involved with books when I was younger. There were no books in the house. There was no music in the house. There was no real culture in the house.

H M: No Bible?

W A: There was a Bible, but at a certain point, I stopped relating to the Bible.

H M: Your family was religious?

W A: They were very religious, but for some reason I turned away. I was not interested in being just a regular type of person. I was observing the regular, churchgoing people, and I could see that they just look at what you wear, what you drive. They're not interested in anything of value.

H M: It was about status?

W A: It was about a secondary status, basically, because the Black people are preoccupied with their secondary status. That's what's so bad about what I call these picture book publications.

H M: Like *Ebony*?

W A: Exactly. I went to a beautiful place in the Leimert district called Congo Square where they have a lot of interesting old memorabilia, and I picked up one of these old *Ebony* magazines from 1954, and they are exactly the same, the pictures look exactly the same, the people look exactly the same . . .

H M: As now?

W A: And the stories were exactly the same.

H M: The formula. This person is successful. Look at the car. Look at the clothes. Look at the shoes!

W A: And look at the way they carry themselves in the world, as a secondary person.

H M: E. Franklin Frazier wrote the book on that.

W A: They're completely trapped in this because they can look down on people who don't have as many material possessions. This is the rule among the supposedly successful Blacks.

H M: You were alienated from that.

W A: Oh, I just saw it as absolutely ridiculous, and I still do, even more so. In fact, it's become a danger to the people who are sound asleep within that. You'll have these large congregations and these successful people who drive up to church in their showcase cars. With all the money going into these churches—and in a city like Los Angeles you'll find tons of churches—but at the same time in the same communities you'll find the dope and the gangs. So what's the point?

H M: A moment ago you said there wasn't much to read at home, so how did you shift gears into being a reader and writer? In another conversation, you told me about a particular experience you had in school with one of your teachers.

W A: I had a problem with reading and confidence. I was just a young child, and you know they would force you to read, and the class would always be divided in groups: the top group, the middle group, the lower group. I was always in the bottom group, and I just couldn't get it. In retrospect I realize that I was just too young.

H M: People forget how hard it is to learn to read.

W A: It's very difficult learning how to read, and English is not easy. So

I'm six years old, my mom is coming to the school, the teacher is worried. I heard a fellow speaking late one night on KPFK, who said that young African-American boys tend to get their reading skills together around the age of eight-and-a-half, and that's exactly what happened to me. This particular teacher got me going. He got me to the point where I knew what I was doing. I was okay, and from then on I was absolutely fine. It was like I was healed. For me I think it was just the right time. It wasn't too late, it was just right. I was pressured to get there, but I got it, and that's all you need really, is just to learn to read. Then you can go use the libraries. If you want to be a physicist or astronomer, something like that, you do need special training, but for poets, I think you can just read books.

H M: Do you remember what the teacher did that made it click for you?

W A: I was just trying really hard, and my mom was really good. She would go and talk with the teacher, and he said, "Keep him working at this." I don't know how it happened, but I began to understand what I saw. I can't tell you exactly when.

H M: And your mom was helping you at home?

W A: Not particularly. No.

H M: But you knew she was concerned.

W A: She was concerned, yes.

H M: Did it make a difference that it was a male teacher?

W A: Maybe so, but if so, it was something unconscious. I think I had just reached the point where I could deal with this.

H M: You were ready.

W A: Yes, and I found out that so many kids get lost. They just miss it.

H M: Because the teacher has a schedule, and expects them to be on that schedule . . .

W A : This system of education doesn't take into account the inner needs of the individual.

H M : So once you got it, how did things change for you?

W A : After that, I was able to do really well with spelling and reading. I remember a report I did on the Aztecs, when I was about eleven years old, and I would check out books on astronomy, but I was mostly interested in baseball. I found out that looking at all these statistics, and the different athletes and their different characters, I was learning things that I didn't know I was learning. From that point on I was really confident about reading and doing what I had to do.

H M : So your writing started . . .

W A : Writing did not start at all until much, much later. No, I was not one of those kids who are writing poems when they are five and ten. I had an idea of writing a book about baseball. That would keep me going. I did write a little story around that time. It was about a pit, and a revolt of these slaves coming out of the pit. They were not Black slaves as such, but they were slaves nevertheless. I had elaborate names for the king and all these individuals who were in revolt, coming up out of the pit. When I saw a picture by the Brazilian photographer Salgado of miners trying to haul up gold out of an abyss, I thought about that little story I'd written as a child, but that's the only thing I wrote back then. About nine or ten years later, I read a book about Rimbaud . . . and I thought, that's me. So I sat at a table, and I wrote my first poem.

H M : At this point, you're in high school?

W A : No, no it was way after high school. I developed after that point, and I found that I just had a natural ability for language. I don't know how; it just comes to me. I would even create words. It got to a state where I was writing two or three poems a day.

HM: Were they for yourself? What were you doing with them?

WA: They were for me. A close friend of mine—Majied Mahadi—we would study together.[1] It was like a workshop, like the Charles Mingus workshop. You were on your own, but there was a fierce competition between us. In a positive way we were pushing each other. We would write together. I'd read to him, and he'd read to me. He was brilliant; he had a philosophical edge. He was Black. By then I'd been reading Garcia Lorca, Kaufman, Aimé Césaire. Before that I'd been involved in political activity. I'd been exposed to world culture, the Chinese and Cuban revolutions, the writings of Marx and Engels.

HM: So there was a political as well as an aesthetic base?

WA: Right, but also, deeper than that, I was more entranced by the character of these individuals.

HM: As human beings, as thinkers?

WA: The power, the magnetism, the force they had coming out of them. It lifts you out of this provincial, quotidian environment in which people pay bills and buy automobiles, and show off their accoutrements. When I saw the book on Rimbaud, it pulled it all together. I thought, now I can work on my own power.

HM: So when did you start to think of yourself and your writing in terms of publishing, or in terms of a larger community beyond the buddy system you'd worked out with your philosopher friend?

WA: We were thinking about that all along. That was a community, the cell of a community. As a poet, right away you're isolated, which can be dangerous because you're young at it, and you're dealing with hostile circumstances as a poet.

HM: Because it's hard to earn a living?

WA: Not only that.

HM: People not caring what you do?

WA: Exactly. Which is worse. It's very intense, but I did get into a couple of special classes at UCLA. The teacher was a very conventional, very conservative poet, but he saw my work, and he took me aside, and in those classes I began to develop and find out what I didn't know. So from writing all those poems every day, I went down to none. At certain points I would ask myself, "Am I really a poet? Yes, I am." I was feeding myself intellectually, finding all of the things that I work with now.

HM: So being in the poetry class actually stopped you for a while.

WA: Exactly. You have to cross the desert.

HM: He was talking about traditional form?

WA: Form—and I had to decide in my own mind how I would work with world knowledge in an original manner, whether it was geography, astronomy . . .

HM: So he had you thinking about how poetry processes knowledge.

WA: I had myself thinking about that. The experience I got in that class was a spur to my self-criticism.

HM: At that point, when was that?

WA: I was just getting out of high school, and I was going into another deep depression because—the word liminal comes up—you're in a gulf, you're between in-between. You're not quite ready to put the work out, and I knew I was completely different than what we call "Black poetry." In fact, I wasn't even interested in that. Because they just give you a little area to live in. So here's your church, here's your poetry.

HM: You saw "Black poetry" as a limitation.

WA: Definitely as a limitation.

H M : Because of the conventions, the themes, the subject matter?

W A : That, and because I knew what Césaire had done, and a little later I'd discovered Wifredo Lam.

H M : So the problem was poetry in the U.S.? African-American poetry?

W A : The African-American condition of poetry.

H M : At that time had you read someone like Tolson, or . . . ?

W A : I looked at Tolson, not as deeply as I could have, should have, even to this moment, but I did know that there were poets like Jean Toomer that I could definitely work with. There are current writers like Leon Forrest, or Calvin Hernton. I think these people are brilliant. There's that level, and then there's the other level. We can write this and get it published , because it's got the formula. I'd read Césaire's "Return to My Native Land," and I'd seen Bob Kaufman's work. This was quite amazing stuff. I knew that Kaufman had not done the conventional move either. I found out that he'd spent time in Los Angeles as a caterer at the Beverly Hills or Bel Air Hotel. He just decided one day he wanted to be a poet, and he left the job. I just published an essay on Kaufman. It just came out in *Conjunctions* ["The Footnotes Exploded," included in this volume].

H M : That's great, I want to read it. So this transitional period is between your leaving UCLA and . . .

W A : And trying to work in the world, and not being able to do it very well, because I'm consumed with trying to find my own language. Every moment was consumed for me totally. I could not rest. I wasn't stable at all. I would work but, just as I am now, I was never much concerned with practical things.

H M : Poetry comes first.

W A : Poetry always comes first. Period. I also began writing tales and stories, and I discovered drawing because I'd also been studying the arts on my own. Discovering that Garcia Lorca drew gave me the inspiration to just go ahead and draw. In the past three or four months, I've been drawing on any piece of paper I get. I've done about fifty or sixty drawings.

H M : Like the drawings included in *The Stratospheric Canticles*?

W A : Those are old drawings, but I do plan on publishing a book of these more recent drawings.

H M : How do you see the relationship between the writing and the drawing, or is there a particular way you'd relate one to the other?

W A : I do relate them. I'm semi-ambidextrous.

H M : You can use either hand to write or draw?

W A : No, I write and draw everything with the right hand. What I mean is that psychologically the drawing feels like I'm left-handed, and it releases me.

H M : I'm right-handed, very right-dominant, but when I try drawing with the left hand, it's very liberating.

W A : Very liberating, the line is very liberating. For me the line creates color. When I draw with graphite, or with the pen, I can actually see different colors in the different lines I draw, although I am only using one color.

H M : Synaesthesia. Another connection to Rimbaud, his poem "Voyelles."

W A : One needs vision. That's more important than scholarship.

H M : But you have both. You've taught yourself a great deal, and you've also had access to formal education.

W A : You need to know your dominant strength. For me what's important is the psychic field. It's an unlimited area one can work in, if you want to go into a world that is not provincial. You know Wifredo Lam was told he had to make art for the tourists, but he said he wouldn't do that. The people had to come to his level. He wasn't being elitist.

HM: Right, it's not condescending. It's actually giving the people credit for being at the artist's level, or believing they're capable of getting there.

WA: As an artist, you seem to be isolated, but you're joining up with greater forces beyond your provincial area.

HM: Okay, I wanted to find out when you started to publish. Could you give a brief account of your publishing history?

WA: I started in the early 1980s. I'd met Clayton Eshleman [editor of the literary journal *Sulfur*], and he suggested that I send some work to *River Styx*, "and tell them I told you to send it." That was it. They published this poem I'd written, "Mountain Slopes Swimming In Detroit." So I began to publish. I published with them again, and one day I received a letter from Nathaniel Mackey, out of the absolute blue: "Would you send something to Hambone?" We've been corresponding since then.

HM: He'd seen this poem?

WA: He'd seen my work around, and he was interested. I had at that point started a book, which I still have around the house. It's a group of letters. It's like his fiction, but I didn't know that he was writing a book like that. I had one book like that, called *Letters to Rosa*. He published a long piece of it in *Hambone*. Basically, he's been great. He's been publishing all of my fiction, and Clayton over the years has been publishing the poetry in *Sulfur*. I've found my way through all these genres of writing on my own. A few years ago I found that I could write essays, so now I have a large collection of essays. I'm continuing to add to it. In fact, I just completed an essay on Mackey, which is going to be published in *Callaloo*, in the next year or so. It was a difficult essay to do. He's a very brilliant and tough writer to work with. I think one has to take time to evolve, and it's very difficult to evolve as a writer because we're in a society that tells us to be complete at every moment, and to rush things along.

HM: Do you feel now that you're coming into your own? Didn't these two books—*Asia & Haiti* (Sun and Moon Press) and *The Stratospheric Canticles* (Pantograph Press)—didn't they come out in the same year? 1995?

WA: Yes, 1995. I have work that I show, and work that I haven't shown yet. There's book after book after book. I've written at least nineteen books now.

HM: Nineteen books, and how much of that is published?

WA: Three more are on the way out, so that'll make half a dozen or so.

HM: So there's a backlog.

WA: I've got ideas. Every day I come up with new ones.

HM: You're writing all the time.

WA: I just finished my third play just about two weeks ago. I hadn't planned on it coming this soon, but it just came out.

HM: So you've got poetry, novels, essays, and drama. You're covering the genres.

WA: There are also aphorisms and tales, and there's a book of philosophy coming out. I do that, too, but at this point, I want to work just with the visual arts for the next half year or so. For the past couple of years I've been working on a very large novel . . . and there are other works to get out. There's also another quite large project, a poem that I've written to Philip Lamantia.

HM: Let me ask about language, because many Black writers, not just

African Americans, but also Caribbean writers, and to some extent African writers as well have dealt with the problem of language, the European language, whatever it is—in our case, English—that one feels alien in the language, one feels uncomfortable, or feels somehow excluded from it. It's a feeling that the language doesn't belong to us even though we learn it the same way everybody else learns it. Especially in this country where so many people have been immigrants who had to learn English and forget another language. That in fact is a typical American experience, although we know that some groups did not immigrate but were appropriated as labor, or their lands were appropriated, so their relationship to English is more overtly coercive. We're talking about a typical American experience, for everyone but the English-speaking colonists. African Americans have been here longer than most immigrant groups, yet it still seems that Black people, more than anyone else, retain the historical trace of coercion. Black writers continue to speak of this discomfort with the European language, and to feel it necessary to create or validate an alternative or parallel language that is racially and culturally marked as a Black language. Or to master English for the purpose of cursing the master, you know, the Calibanization of English. I'd argue that American English is not a European or "white" language. It's a miscegenated language because of our linguistic contribution and inventiveness.

WA: At this point, I'm very comfortable with English. I have no problems with it. I am concerned with using language like Césaire to turn the world upside down. Sartre said that no white man could write French like Césaire wrote French, and Césaire deliberately chose to write in French rather than Creole, in order to subvert the limitations placed on him as a Black writer.

H M : It's claiming the language, but using it in a way that only you can use it, and that does not necessarily mean carving out a racially marked dialect.

W A : Only speaking for myself, I don't need another dialect. I find words every day that I've never used before. I might use words that I create, words that didn't exist in the language.

H M : You said to me in another conversation that sometimes you write as if the words are translated from another language.

W A : When I was reading Deleuze and Guattari, they discuss this, which was something I'd already discovered in myself. It's not that I know these other languages, like Spanish or Italian, but I can feel their rhythms, although I'm writing in English. Writing a foreign language within your own language creates another language.

H M : Also, you could say that poetry is never really the standard language. Poetry exceeds the standard dialect, because the poet will break the rules of grammar, violate the conventions, twist the logic of the standard language. Just as subversive as the fugitive slave stealing literacy, the poetry heads toward the edges and boundaries of language.

W A : I've gone to the point of creating new words. I can hear words that don't exist. They're close to words that exist, but they're different.

H M : How do you feel about the institutionalization of an African-American canon of literature? Of course it represents a monumental achievement—the writing, the scholarship, even the literary politics—but how do you feel about the fact that the canon will inevitably exclude certain writers, such as yourself, while including others?

W A : I don't need it. I'm what you could call a maroon. I'm a psychic maroon.

HM: Marooned from the mainstream, as well as from any academically and pedagogically oriented canon?

WA: Absolutely, from both. Both of them join up, at one point or another.

HM: Do you feel marooned also from the avant-garde?

WA: I'm not interested in that as some kind of activity to pursue, although I am planning a book of concrete poetry, and other books I don't have a notion of yet. I'm more interested in the creative activity than in some kind of movement. Not even a surrealist movement. **HM:** So you're outside of any movement, but would you find alliances in particular movements?

WA: You find alliances across the spectrum. A lot of possible alliances haven't even been worked out yet.

HM: I want to ask you some particular questions about Asia & Haiti. I'm interested in how you feel it fits into the rest of your work, because from what I've seen of your work, it seems to be a departure, in terms of its overt political engagement, but maybe you'll want to comment on that later. What seems continuous in your work is the use of a complex sentence structure, a hyperhypotactic sentence. As a grammatical and syntactical structure, each poem appears as an accumulation of parallel coordinated and subordinated clauses and phrases constituting a potentially unending hypotactic sentence. It's a contrast to the current emphasis, in some circles of formally innovative poets, on the disjunctive, paratactic "new sentence." Your work is going in a different direction, with a different kind of sentence.

WA: Well, first of all I never think about theories when I'm writing. I don't think about how my work fits, or doesn't fit, into some dominant formula, or some avant-garde condition. The words "Asia" and "Haiti" came to me, as words will just come to me. Normally poems come up from inside and the titles come later. In this case the title came first. I did know something about Tibet. It was utterly fascinating to me, and I found an interesting book on Haiti. I thought: This is interesting subject matter; let's go with it. I used the books that I've footnoted in my text. I used an old book, *Lhasa and Its Mysteries*. It's from an old British colonial expedition, but the information in it is hard to find anywhere else, about the animals, the brown-shouldered tiger cat, the practices of the monks, and the old Bon religion before Buddhism. I'm not following his tack, but I'm getting the information that will allow me insight into the region. This is the kind of travel that I do. I'm not one of those writers who has to go to a place. I tend to travel in situ, but the way I intuit most times travel is not required.

HM: You travel in your mind, with the book as a vehicle.

WA: Exactly. I'm not going to pack a bunch of supplies—I mean, what was good for Lewis and Clark and the early explorers is not what I need.

HM: Well, not to get too theoretical, but do you feel that the type of sentence you use is particularly suited to include and accumulate information from the diverse sources that you process in your poetry?

WA: That probably comes up through surrealism and automatic writing. There's a certain state of mind that one can get into, where one actually goes, and everything one touches begins to erupt. I wrote the Haiti poem first. I would write those verses on the bus, and at the job, and at home. I wrote anywhere, anytime. The Haiti poem was finished in about a month, and the Asia poem, honestly, in two weeks.

HM: Wow! You were inspired.

WA: The Asia poem I'm particularly fond of, because for the first time, I was able to use the Occidental College library near my home. It was amenable, quiet, and I was able to take my books up there. Take my work and just go at it, day after day. When I can sit and concentrate like that, writing is no problem. It did take a synthesis of a lot of information, and an understanding of how this was going to work. You have to find a resonance for these words to come.

H M : What is your sense of how information is processed in a poetic form, and also how do you incorporate into the poetry the lexicons, the diverse and arcane vocabularies that seem to come from this research, this background reading that you do?

W A : I know this, that the poet has to be infused with the plasma, the river of poetry, so that the river sweeps through, and it takes up everything in its path. It all becomes part of the river. The poetry is flowing so strongly that it can go in any direction. That's what allows me to go in any direction I feel.

H M : Okay, I wanted to ask about—I noticed as I was reading, that there are certain lines that are metaphors for the Haitian people and their oppression, lines that provide what I can clearly read as metaphorical images of the anonymous dead and the spiritual world of the African diaspora like: "we the first gatherers of wool" [72], "plankton armies empowered by anger with a special knowledge of torture" [76], or "a collective force of burning ink" [119], which is more abstract, but still gives a sort of picture that I can relate to the history and politics of Haiti. It seems to me that the clarity of these lines emerges from the obscurity of other lines that are less concerned with conveying to the reader any particular image or information, for example: "as to answer according to numerical compacting / we have no plausibility / no instinctive message to convey / as to the alvine / or the abstract / the nigrescent human field / is like a wayward carbolic / or a venomous predacity / with a less & less refined devolvement." Sometimes there are torrents of words, without those words having any necessity to create or suggest an image, or to describe any referential reality. One of the French theorists, Greimas, defines a type of metaphor in which the vehicle has more reality than the tenor. He calls it a "negative complex isotopy." Then there is something he calls the "ectopic" image, a purely aesthetic use of images, in which terms are only vehicles, with no function other than to suggest "something else." The image only refers to itself. There's only language referring to itself. It's language for the sake of language, or maybe language for the pleasure and accomplishment of language.

WA: That's the reality of what people call "the surreal," to be able to fly without pedestrian manacles. It's the imagination taking off. There are levels where the mind can go—it's like Egyptian science, that deals not only with the visible world, but the invisible world as well. When you're dealing with the surreal, when it organically vibrates—this is what Césaire said about surrealism—it's perfectly conjunctive with my understanding of an African world view. It deals with the visible and the invisible. So for me the invisible is something that not only takes place in a subconscious realm, but also in a supraconscious realm as well as a conscious realm. It's back to that river again. You're dealing with a triple mind instead of a single mind. Most people look at the world with this single, literal mind, which is part of the scape of the mind, but it is definitely not the end of the mind. In fact the mind is infinity at the supra levels, which the Western cultures have never really valued.

HM: Transcending the self, the ego, the particularity of the individual . . .

W A : Exactly.

H M : . . . which could be achieved by means of meditation, trance, spirit possession?

W A : Exactly, and for me to get to this point, I'm able, through years of praxis, with language, working in this zone, where I walk around in this state, in a continuous pitch twenty-four hours a day.

H M : So you're using language as an entrance into an altered state of consciousness. **W A :** It is a state of consciousness that I think will be more necessary for the human race. We're getting to the point where the old boundaries are being eroded. We're going to need to go back and go forward at the same time, recovering the old knowledge that the original cultures put into the world. Civilization did not start from a reduction, but an expansion. Our systems of knowledge and education have to recover the expansiveness of the first mind. Our minds have been reduced. The Hubble telescope has given us a glimpse of infinity of which we are part.

H M : Okay, I want to go back again to *Asia & Haiti*. When you visited my graduate seminar, I suggested that your intent, in placing the two poems together, using two Third World cultures—and I noted that there is no "white oppressor" in either of these poems—that those poems take seriously the power that is invested in the hands of "Third World" people, for good or ill.

W A : Yes, it's true. In the African-American context, we're so used to seeing ourselves in that secondary role that we talked about at the beginning. Mao and Duvalier were powerful men. Heads of state with real armies and real power. This is what upsets the European powers, and it's why, after the Haitians had their revolution and kicked out the French, they never got any positive international intervention. That was the beginning of their cycle of poverty. But, if you look at the populations of the earth, the majority of countries of the world are run by non-white people, because the majority of the people in the world are not white.

H M : It also seems to me that in juxtaposing the two poems, it is possible to read one in terms of the other. By putting the two poems together, you suggest for the reader a correspondence, a parallel experience of looking at the political situation, and also in looking at the world from the Third World perspective. In both poems there's a model of magic, from the Buddhist chanting, the mind power or word power, to the Voudou vengeance of the dead Haitians who are imagining or witnessing the torture of the Duvaliers, in another world. I also saw this as a model for the poet, particularly because both poems have a collective speaker, a "we" that seems to include the poet, and even the reader. It is "we" whose power is "a collective force of burning ink." The power of words, the power of the curse, invective, spell, chant. The magical revenge of the Haitians against the Duvaliers, and the magical warfare of the exiled Tibetan Buddhist monks against the Chinese Communist invaders.

W A : I agree with that level of warfare, because in order to bring the elements of the total mind together, one has to escape the bifurcation of the mind, the reduction of the mind to only one of its aspects, its reduction to something that can only work on the literal level. I think of the magic as working slowly like medicine. It's a slow-motion magic that's going on even as we speak.

H M : So, do you definitely see your work as being ideologically engaged? Or is it these poems more than the others?

W A : No, I don't see these poems as any strict ideological formation. First of all, they are poems. If one is writing about these regions, that's part of the region. The magic is part of that, but also the recent political conditions of the modern world, after 1950. Specifically 1950 and 1957. Duvalier came to power in 1957.

HM: To the extent that there is an engagement with ideology—yes, these are poems whose main purpose may be aesthetic or spiritual, with an agenda of consciousness raising—it also seems that the poems critique the ideologies of both communism and capitalism. The situation in Haiti is a byproduct of capitalism.

WA: Yes, I find that neither system can fully integrate the other levels of the mind that we've talked about. Both systems require the mind's reduction to a small, regimenting mind.

HM: Because both are focused on the means of production, and on the material world?

WA: Basically, that's it.

HM: That's what unites communism and capitalism.

WA: That's what I'm talking about. The whole Cold War was based on how many tanks and rockets does each side have.

HM: So the entire human consciousness, and the levels above and below normal consciousness, are all subordinated to one's relation to the means of production, one's labor or one's capital?

WA: One's labor or one's capital. People in their daily lives, in all their moments—their minds are governed by this.

HM: Let me ask how you would relate *Asia & Haiti* to your other works, such as *The Stratospheric Canticles*, which it seems to me goes in other directions?

WA: Well, it's working in the same—I'm working with the same level of mind.

H M : In *The Stratospheric Canticles* there's a kind of roaming encyclope-
dic energy for accumulating categories of knowledge. Poems dealing
with the natural world, animals, and the title poem that deals with visual arts and painting. It seems to me less politically charged.

W A : Charged? It's charged. It may not be about some place that you find
on a map, but it's that intermediate world that one finds when one
opens up the mind. It's there when I talk about world painting, Miró,
El Greco, Jackson Pollock. These people existed. They worked in
these other shimmering dimensions. Every work that I do is charged,
but different. Some people reach a level of quality, and continue to do
that same kind of work. That's fine. Some people just write poetry.
That's fine. I have another idea. I have different ideas all the time for
books. I just came up with another idea for a book that I can't do right
now because I've got too many other things I'm trying to do.

H M : So when that happens, what would you do? Take notes, put it on the
back burner, or you'd just leave it hanging?

W A : I'd just leave it. Or like Miró, he'd have different canvases he'd be
working on, all at different points on the way to completion.

H M : You work on multiple projects at the same time, and go from one to
the other? Or you concentrate on one?

W A : I concentrate on one, and try to finish it; but at the same time, I do
have all these ideas for other books.

H M : I want to ask some questions about audience. Do you write with a
particular audience in mind, or do you think you need to? Or do you
think the work creates its audience, or finds its audience, or the audience finds the work? In general, what do you think about your relationship to an audience?

W A : The work finds an audience.

HM: That's how it's been?

WA: I don't do any type of promotion of my work at all.

HM: But you are doing readings now.

WA: I do readings, talks, lectures; but people ask me to do them. I don't ask them, "can I do this?" They ask me, and I do them. That way you can burn your way through rock into the light. I'm not sending out a bunch of faxes, or knocking on doors.

HM: So you're not concerned at all about a Black audience?

WA: No, because I know plenty of Black people who read my work.

HM: That is a part of your audience.

WA: Exactly. I have no problem with my identity. You can get to a certain level of consciousness, which is available to all of the races. In every race you want to work at the higher level. Whites who know only whites are ghettoized and provincial. These separations are limitations on the mind.

HM: We all tend to be separated into our various boxes.

WA: I just want to throw the box away.

HM: So do you see poetry as a means of doing that, of bringing people together, if poets are writing for the sake of a higher consciousness rather than for the sake of race or identity?

WA: Well, when one is working with consciousness, one is always working with one's identity and one's race, because that is part of one's consciousness. I would never separate them. I'm not a European, and what I am is there in the rhythms of my work. It's there in what I feel and who I am. There's no question that a Black person is writing this. A Black person's experience in the Western world is different form a white person's experience.

HM: So you don't feel you need to make any special effort to write in any special language to make it evident that you are an African-American because you feel that your identity permeates your work in any case.

WA: Naturally. Your identity is a given point from which you can explore.

HM: By doing that you also expand the arena for what "Black writing" is?

WA: For what writing is, period!

HM: Oh yes, of course. I mean that the box we were talking about, that Black writers are put into, that you ignore the box. Then you're able to do what you want to do, without having to worry about your identity.

WA: That's correct. Everybody's talking about being free and being liberated. Well, isn't that the point, to be liberated to do and feel as you are? That's the point!

WILL ALEXANDER

A PROFOUND INVESTIGATION

Conducted by Marcella Durand

MARCELLA DURAND: It's funny—I was looking for your phone number, and then you called me. I thought, how fitting for Will Alexander.

WILL ALEXANDER: It's interesting. [Clairvoyance] works out of almost
a blind state in terms of the rational context, or a conscious perspective. It doesn't seem to have a clue, and then all of a sudden it arrives
on the conscious plane.

MD: How much does clairvoyance figure into your writing?

WA: I'd say a lot because I tend to pick up energy and areas of knowledge
that I did not know much about consciously. When I go back and check
them out, it's absolutely accurate. I read and I look at the synecdoche.
The yogi Swami Vivekananda[1] pointed out that he'd go through a book
like that and get the very essence of it. It is not an excuse, but it is a
way of working with the text that is supposedly unconventional. It's
something that Edward de Bono talks about repeatedly in his book
Lateral Thinking, that there are different approaches to the mind,
rather than this knowledge adds up to this knowledge adds up to this
knowledge. There are other ways of approaching reality.

M D : You've described the I as a bit of "carbon" released outward into experience. Is that what you're talking about as a process of knowledge?
Releasing an identity that can be anything?

W A : It's true. This piece of carbon can be an eye, a human being, a leopard or a remora—there are many ways of speaking through animals.
In my latest group of poems, there is one with a voice whose energy
is water, but water on another planet. It's called "Water on New Mars"
and the water on New Mars is the water of a parallel Mars.

M D : Where is the parallel Mars?

W A : It's in a transvicinity. Over and beyond vicinity. I'm actually locating
and exploring this water in this zone of transvicinity. I do mention
specific locales on Mars, and they become proto-locales and supra-
locales sometimes, but they are locales in themselves, like the Olympus Mons.[3]

M D : So it's a combination of physical locales and the realm of the mind?

W A : Intersecting, because that goes back to the triple mind, the supraconscious, the conscious, and the subconscious. In other words, this
spills out into all of reality, probably into every zone of the universe
that one can find, although we don't really know the mysteriousness
of the universe. There may be areas that don't even have carbon-
based life. But for this particular level of exploration, the carbon par-
ticle is quite apt.

M D : You've said you don't travel much physically, but you're a great mental traveler.

W A : The imagination has to ignite the process, wherever the base is. That
said, I find that because the mind goes at such a rate, I can almost—as
the old metaphysicians talked about—go directly to Mauritania or to
Haiti, or Canada, or Detroit, or wherever I've been to and then relate

it to the idea of the supra-plane and the physical plane. All of those levels partake of one single substance. The interesting part comes when divisions take place, and separate cuisines, separate psychologies, separate environments come into play—turmoil, political situations, such as in Sri Lanka or Madagascar. I can go there instantaneously. [Gilles] Deleuze talks about that—traveling from your chair. And it works because if I had to travel as fast as my mind was working, I couldn't do it.

MD: Right, and it saves on plane tickets.

WA: Right! I mean, that's the way I work. I know William Vollman talks about having to write his books in the next few years because he won't be able to physically take himself to all these environments that he goes to.

MD: It's not so much that you're using mimetic language—that you go somewhere and try to reflect it in words—rather, you're creating something as you perceive it. I wanted to ask you how you research . . .

WA: Again, by synecdoche and by predilection and going through a book almost as Tristan Tzara would open up a dictionary. I can read four or five passages out of a book and begin to explore in my mind. Of course, the accuracy of the vocabulary and the accuracy of what I'm talking about have to be explored, too. I'm not going to just say anything. I want to be very site-specific if it's something on Mars or on another planet. I will read in the particular area I need to read on as early as I can and get the logistics, then let the imagination explore and create, as though that part of the universe reflected the whole of the universe with the motion of living that had gone into creating that part of the universe, then manifest it in language. So in that sense I'm joining the creation of the universe, but in my own particular way, which is opening and opening and opening, which is not a literal reality, but an experiential reality. It remains fresh and it remains fresh and it remains fresh. When I've explored it, I've gone through it, I'm finished with it, it's published and put into the world, and it remains in that state of motion.

M D : How do you revise?

W A : I rehear something maybe once or twice, mostly just once. I handwrite everything and then I get on the typewriter or computer, and I hear other levels and that's my finished product.

M D : In your interview with Harryette Mullen,[4] you say Rimbaud was an early influence. When did you decide to become a poet?

W A : When I saw that it was the only thing I could really do in this life— like Bud Powell, playing the piano. What he wanted to do and what he could organically do were inextricably linked. I had lived an intense emotional life up to that point and the mediums out of which that emotion could express itself had been inadequate. Around that period, I found this little book on Rimbaud and I read it and I felt it was me. I was able to begin to explore a medium that hitherto was unknown to me. At that point, I felt it more than I knew it. I felt poetry. I literally felt it. I had felt poetry when listening to the great jazz musicians, really deeply. When I heard John Coltrane play, I couldn't believe it. It was that good.

M D : I've often thought if I could sit George Bush down and make him listen to "A Love Supreme," his mind would be opened . . .

W A : Those types are very resistant to reality. They are trees in a hurricane. Since they don't bend, they ultimately break. They don't have any flexibility. When I listen to this music, there's this incredible flexibility. A combination of flexibility and formal sophistication, emotional and technical accuracy. I remember as a child I saw an American doctor's wife on the evening news in attendance at a Haitian voodoo ceremony. They showed her swaying—she had to walk out because she said it was taking her over. Breton had that same sense of the ceremonies, in the 1940s. There's an imaginal power that comes from all over the world, but particularly from the former colonies in the Southern hemisphere, energy that started the knowledges in the world, which is basically a right-brain knowledge. In the early kingdoms, the right brain was the dominant factor. I'm thinking specifically of Egypt, but it did not preclude profound investigation of the arts, of the sciences, of mathematics. There's a perceptive writer on that area, Beatrice Lumpkin.[5] Cheikh Anta Diop[6] talks about this area, as well. I'm coming from an energy and experience that predates the Western idea of reality that has been discredited in the past 500 years or so.

M D : You write quite a bit about Kemet.[7] Could you talk a little more about what that pre-Greek idea of reality was?

W A : Kemet means "black soil," and simultaneously refers to Black people. For me the "black soil" refers to both the physical climate, as well as the climate of the mind. [In ancient Kemet] if you were studying geology, astronomy, poetry, you got into the whole activity of the cosmos as a whole rather than a part. Knowledge had its own dynamic. Say I was studying the activity, the motion of the land in geology, I would understand it not as a secular or separable activity. Another analogy is to look at how an orchestra is set up—the oboes, the flutes, the piccolos. In some pieces, certain instruments dominate, but the flow of the whole orchestra propels that particular domination at that moment.

MD: When you write, do you feel it adds an essential movement to the symphony, even if it's not read by everyone?

WA: Absolutely. If you move something on earth, it affects something else in the cosmos. These knowledges that I'm talking about are echoed through different times in different individuals. We're not born to set up an artificial division between what happens in the West and what happens in the Southern climes, although there are essential differences. You have people like Roger Bacon[8] or Robert Grosseteste,[9] Bacon's teacher, who talked about light and elemental conjunctions of reality, which is pre-Leonardo. Roger Bacon was the first person in the West to talk about a flying machine, not Leonardo. But the first manned glider flight took place in Cordoba in 875, invented by the engineer, Abbas Ibn Firmas.

MD: Leonardo wrote quite a bit on light in his notebooks.

WA: Grosseteste preceded that by a couple of hundred years. They were persecuted by the church because the church is based on a separable condition. Basically [Grosseteste and Bacon] were coming out of Moorish culture. As for Leonardo and his writings on light it was Alhazen centuries prior to Grosseteste and Leonardo who made "discoveries on the physiology of vision," and on the theory of reflection and refraction of light.

MD: Oh yes, you've talked about the Moors and how as scientists they had discovered things very early.

WA: They actually created the Renaissance in Europe, but they're never given credit because of their religion and their color. They held the Iberian Peninsula for 500 years. It was the only place where there was an organization of knowledge at that time. After the Roman Empire fell, there was a dispersion, a tremendous dispersion. Texts were held in monasteries, but there was never a concordance of sustained exploration for centuries. This was pointed out in an astronomy seminar I used to go to many ages ago. I'd go on these retreats with Dr. E. C. Krupp who runs the planetarium here.[10] One day we talked about the Crab Nebula and why it hadn't been recorded in Europe, but was recorded by the Chinese and the Moors [in 1054]. One of the astronomers there said, and I'm paraphrasing, "Well, maybe there was a fog over Europe and they couldn't see it." In other words, you have to have a system of organization to create knowledge. You have to have some sort of consistency with reality in order to organize and understand, say, water systems or water tables. There were hundreds of bookstores in Cordoba, and the seeds for the modern university were sown there. Jewish scholars, Christian scholars, Islamic scholars—it was one of our last hopes, because the three religions [pursued] knowledge in a way that was harmonious without losing their individuality. After the fall of the Moors, Christians began to dismantle the bathhouses, to disrupt and persecute and destroy. It coincides with the mounting fervor of the Inquisition and the beginning of the slave trade. Hermeticism seemed to be lost in Europe. It went underground and went underground and went underground.

M D : Why do you think these things happened at the same time, the Inquisition and the slave trade?

W A : I don't want to give some kind of answer to that. Things coalesce in history and there seems to be some sort of a tie that takes place. You have an idea that other people who are Asian or peoples of color, or people of other psychological persuasions, like Bacon, were no longer necessary. The internal state was superseded by external reasoning and definition began to accrue in terms of outer form. Exterior perfection was exalted, inner form dissolved, or was reduced to a minor rhetoric. Malraux points out the difference between the image of a 9th-century Christ and one of a 15th-century Christ. The former is less technical, but charged with interior feeling; the latter is commanding by means of its painterly virtuosity. The inner reverberation is replaced by technical expertise.

MD: What do you think about the shutdown of the Hubble Space Telescope?

WA: I think it's a disaster. [The Hubble] is an opportunity to explore things that really and truly are unknown. We don't even know about everything on this planet. We don't even know about ourselves. [The Hubble] is a gift. The problem is that we don't have a sustained society, but a truncated one, that moves from fragment to fragment.

MD: Do you see the poet as having a mission to discover wholeness again?

WA: I wouldn't just say the poet, but also the mathematician and the scientist. I think mathematics and science in the created sense come out of the same spirit. We've gotten to this extreme level of separation where we have to have conflict. Once in a while, a few conjunctions appear.

MD: I think astronomy is one way to restore people to their proper sizes.

WA: Astronomy does, because it is so strange. We've come to this point that when you look at astronomy, it explodes completely into another zone. None of our ideas of God—how can I put it?—none of our ideas about religion are capable of understanding it. The shadow system that they're exploring now—dark matter, what put that there? Stellar nurseries in Serpens with cloud towers six million trillion miles long. Yet the movement of life found there is the same energy that's populating this zone.

M D : Have you heard this theory that the chemical involved in the Big Bang is the same as when people fall in love?

W A : Basically what love is, is conjunction. What I think plagues the West is this whole idea of separation. Lots of beings, lots of objects. It's why the ecological situation is such a disaster. I've thought many times about how we can run an economic system without a stable weather system. You can't. Whether you call it global warming or climate change, it will destroy the economic base. A perspicacious 10-year-old can figure that out. I've talked to children and they understand it.

M D : It's not really about money. It doesn't make monetary sense.

W A : It's an ideology. There are other knowledges being explored that are not on the level of the strictly visible. There have been writers in the West who have actively sought this, most notable René Daumal. People like him keep this underground current that goes back to Bacon alive. It's everywhere. Octavio Paz said this current will always be here no matter what name we call it. It will never go away, no matter what the dominant ideology that seeks to prevent its praxis is.

M D : What other poets are you inspired or influenced by? You've mentioned the Surrealists . . .

W A : Oh, there's been so many. Basically, they come from obscure areas. People like Robert Marteau and Dino Campana, Fernando Pessoa's heteronyms. Of course, the Mexican poet Gorostiza, for topical relevance. For the impact he had on the modern world of poetry, Ramon Lopez Velarde. Octavio Paz. Antonin Artaud. Andre Breton. César Vallejo's poems are incredibly exciting and powerful. Also early Williams.

M D : Not later Williams?

WA: Not the Paterson Williams but Hart Crane. Philip Lamantia. Bob— I've been in his presence.

MD: Bob Kaufman?

WA: Yes. We were in the same house together, although Bob was sitting in another room. It was myself, Philip Lamantia, and Neely Cherkovski looking at the original typescript of "The Ancient Rain;" I saw the original form and the original type.

MD: Are you in contact with Philip Lamantia still?

WA: I just called him yesterday. I had finished an incredible experience with the Alice Farley Dance Company. It was amazing—we had dancers, forms, all the incredible costumes she makes, we read the poems of the poet Laurence Weisberg. It was the most unconventional reading because we choreographed it like theatre, music, sound, poetry, dance. It was fortuitous energy. It was recorded and filmed, so we have the document.

MD: I wanted to ask you about your essays. Do you work out philosophical concepts in them that you use later in poetry?

WA: Certain energies come out as poetry, while certain ideas come out as essays. They form into this or that configuration. For me, my initial idea in writing essays is something I came to not right away, but I just found that I needed another way to express myself. I got the idea from photography. When a photographer is out shooting things, he or she finds things that impress him or her instantaneously. For me, an essay is like that—I find something interesting and write about it.

MD: I was particularly intrigued by your essay on Azarian Mathematics.[11]

WA: That was completely something that I created. I would like to get enough knowledge at one point to actually study the symbols of higher mathematics and visualize Azarian Mathematics—mathematics simultaneously strengthened by a powerful visual stimulus. Mathematics and poetry are very, very close in the sense that a theorem or an equation functions as a penetrant calligraphy. Here's a quote from an essay called "Beauty of Mathematics: A Review"[12] on British mathematician Godfrey Harold Hardy: "Everyone knows that mathematicians sometimes speak of perfectly formulated equations as beautiful and are excited by them as are connoisseurs excited by works of art. The present volume will be of great interest and value to estheticians and the sense that it is here for the first time that the beauty of mathematics will be discussed by a mathematician. Professor Hardy's analysis of this beauty is penetrating and illuminating in welcome contrast to the vagueness that is so characteristic of most modern writings on the criteria of beauty in other kinds of art." Here's another quote: "A mathematician like a painter or a poet is a maker of patterns. The mathematician's patterns like the painter's or the poet's must be beautiful. The ideas, like the colors or the words, must fit together in a harmonious way. Beauty is the first test. There is no permanent place in the world for ugly mathematics." This is the way I look at it because as I see it, poetry has to be this beautiful and this accurate.

M D : It reminds me of the Golden Mean.[13] So many painters used it in their work. And what about your artwork, which has patterning in it reminiscent of astronomical or biological patterns? **W A :** That realia of drawing came to me before my first recognizable poems evinced. I had been studying so much of Miró's work that I began to draw a figure in pencil one day and it worked—I've been working that way ever since. Federico Garcia Lorca's drawings gave me the initial impetus to go forward in this direction, simply working with intuition. I've never taken an art class in my life. I've never had a tutor. I'm seriously involved right now in finishing a volume of drawings.

MD: Who is your writing community? Do you have a community in L.A.?

WA: There is a community, people that I know in different parts of the country—yourself, Andrew Joron, Nathaniel Mackey, Philip Lamantia. There's so many of them, I can't tell you. Listen, I'll leave people out, but I know they're there, and they know they're there. And there are some who are not in print, and people reading this interview will have never heard of them. For instance, Jim Henderson. The lifelong conversation I had with him was spectacular. We discussed an integral metaphysics combining the whole of life, sparked by our mutual understanding of Sri Aurobindo. He's passed on now, but he was very vital to me. People like that have been important to me.

MD: Do you correspond with writers in the Caribbean or Tibet?

WA: At this point, I don't. I quite, quite strenuously tried to contact Aimé Césaire. Last spring, I organized a national Surrealist conference, "The Imaginal Present and Future," cosponsored by the French Consulate. I posted contact with Césaire, which they transmitted. We did not get any response. This is unfortunate—I know there may be a language barrier, but that's not insurmountable. I'm thinking about going to Martinique in the not-too-distant future.

MD: People have compared you quite a bit to Césaire—do you feel that's accurate?

WA: Well, in a spiritual sense, yes. What he was doing, and continues to do—there's nothing like it. He'll come up with a phrase and it's like a beautiful breath of oxygen. He was speaking in his "Letter to Maurice

Thorez" about the particulars of the Southern Hemisphere and people of color and the way he put it together was quite extraordinary. There's just nothing like it, the power in the poetry and his *Discourse on Colonialism*. I call it the "big book." It is some 75 pages, but it seems as though one had gone through 300 pages of insight. So, it does feel accurate in that sense, but not in terms of my experience—I'm coming out of another world.

MD: He's very involved with his locale.

WA: Well, I grew up in an urban society. I don't want to make this a pat answer, but I've had to have a big city in order to do the kind of work I do. You need a lot of resources.

MD: And universities?

WA: Universities. I need to travel across an eclectic range. Libraries, bookstores, cinemas, all kinds of metaphysical societies—I've been going to lectures for years. I have an incredible conduit, a man named Roger Weir. He continues to educate with insight after insight as if a current were running through you. Lectures on China, quantum physics, exobiology, Jung. He's given me a lot of information that I've been able to work with over the years. His lectures should be transcribed and published. He has volumes and volumes; you could fill a library with these lectures. People like that, you wouldn't find in many parts of the world. There's so much out here, so much to work with. You work with what you can and you work at your capacity. I understand I have limitations and I have to understand those limitations in order to continue to evolve.

MD: You grew up in L.A.

WA: Yes, yet I've never looked at L.A. as a provincial enclave. There are some poets who defend the region against other regions. There's no need to do that. In fact, that's something I've never adhered to. It's an-tipoetic in the sense that they immure themselves in a desolate topog-raphy. I find this to be incredibly limiting. But the western coast has its own particulars. Many years ago, Jack Wise, the Canadian painter said, and again I'm paraphrasing, "We are looking out at China on the West coast." In the east you're looking at Europe, we're looking at China. The Asiatic influence is incredible. I did customer service for this company, and I've been writing these names down. Incredible long, long, long names. Indian long, Laotian long. Long, long names. I mean, it's unbelievable. My next experience, because I'm gathering all this, is I want to write a novel from the Saxon perspective concern-ing the re-encroachment of peoples of color overrunning the West. The encroachment of the other.

MD: How are you doing that?

WA: It's very complex. I've done some 20 books and I am at this point where—whoa—I have got to assess some of what I've written. I need to work on getting my trilogy of novels out into the world. Spuyten Duyvil is going to put them out late next year under one cover. And then there's another handwritten novel in a duffel bag, called *Diary as Sin*. Douglas Messerli has a novella called *Alien Weaving*. So the Saxon novel would be my fourth attempt, but I'm going to take my time with it because I have other things to do and a lot of things I have to work with. As I said earlier on, I'm going to be working on research-ing and basically being a visual artist for a number of months.

ALCHEMICAL DADA

AN INTERVIEW WITH WILL ALEXANDER

Conducted by Grant Jenkins in Los Angeles in June 2004

GRANT JENKINS: I am actually going to tape what you [are] saying about the recent period, how it's been tough.

WILL ALEXANDER: It has always been such, you know. So we are doing this for possible *Rain Taxi* . . .

GJ: . . . possible *Rain Taxi*, I talked to Eric Lorberer about doing a series of interviews about contemporary experimental African American writers. So I am interviewing, I interviewed Harryette out here in March. I interviewed Mark McMorris in May in DC. Yourself and then Mackey tomorrow and Monday. So hopefully that will become a series. Really, I am doing this is for a larger project and I feel like these interviews are my first step, the beginning of the project and almost a learning phase for . . .

WA: Learning curve?

GJ: Yeah. Frankly there isn't a lot of secondary material on this group. And because I'm working on African American poetry, the first thing I want to admit up front is that I am white and that I am not going to take this authorial voice that "Here's an academic's take on poetry."

One of the strategies I use in the classroom is to let the poetry speak for itself. We read black critics and other people so that my class is multivocal. I've taken that methodology to this project, and I want these interviews to be a primary source, that the poets themselves are talking. I don't know how that is going to shape into a larger critical work at all, but it certainly is my starting point and way in. I think the interviews themselves . . .

W A : Can stand on their own.

G J : Right. And interviews seem to work in this field as a great way to expose people to the work. I know you did an interview in 1997 for *Callaloo*. Was that the last time?

W A : No, there was one other, with Marcella Durand.

G J : You were talking about how things lately have been good. Is that since the *Callaloo* interview or before *Callaloo*.

W A : Well, I've been pretty—in terms of the work, it has been pretty steady. In terms of projects and getting things accomplished. It's been pretty intense.

G J : Does that include your drawings and other . . .

W A : Other aspects. I should have brought more stuff here to show you, but I think I have enough material here in the back here. I have been doing so many things. This is a wonderful part of it, but I'd like to have more time to do more. I've done so many other things in terms of writing, in terms of different types of writing. I did bring some novels I want to show you. And I've been doing pencil drawings and these color fields. I've also been an artist/facilitator for this agency in Los Angeles called Theatre of Hearts/Youth First. It gives arts to at-risk youth in the Los Angeles Region . . .

G J : They called you first?

WA: Yes, they came to me first. I met Sheila Scott-Wilkinson, the Founder/Executive Director. She's also an excellent artist. Her photographs really go deeply. So I've been doing that, and also I've been doing a lot of inner work on my inner workings. I am working right now on what I consider to be a hermetic piece on myself.

GJ: Autobiography?

WA: I wouldn't call it that. Because of the fact that it touches on different layers and implicit quanta. I am not the type to write biography, autobiography of what happened. I do wish I had taken a couple of notes about my day to day experiences over the past five years. It's been very intense. I am doing another project now entailing sports and training. I am trying to catch up with all the money at one time. In the mean time, I have been able to compose two pretty large poems. I have a small excerpt here. It's called the "Concerning the Henbane Bird." I've been feeding off of that in different anthologies and magazines. This excerpt is about ten pages. And I have a companion piece to that which I haven't typed up. It is in handwritten form. It's called "On Solar Physiology." That's still in longhand.

GJ: You compose with paper and pen?

WA: Paper and pen.

GJ: You mentioned they were both long. Have you sort of settled into the long form as your natural poetic form? Most of your work is longer, like *Asia & Haiti*. Even your shorter poems tend to be longer. Do you prefer that long form?

WA: I do prefer it, definitely. But I am not averse to the short poem. I have done two line poems, three line poems. I've done one page poems, nine lines, twelve line, a series of poems that are going to come out in

Green Integer volume in about, if things go well, it should be before the year is over.

GJ: What was the publisher?

WA: Green Integer. Douglas Messerli is doing that.

GJ: It's an anthology?

WA: No, it is a book of mine called *Impulse & Nothingness*, which has been on the burner for some time.

GJ: You've had this idea for a while for this book?

WA: It's been done many years ago. Most of the pieces have been published. It just feels like I've been waiting a while. You know the economics of the small presses. But if you get the right contacts and get input, they do get distributed. Better than the big houses because they lose interest after the first burst. But this way you get a seminal contact point with the editor, the publisher, and you get the seminal contact with your readers.

GJ: So publication has been good for you?

WA: Yes, I've been fortunate almost since the beginning.

GJ: So what's come out since 1997?

WA: The books that you would already know about like [*Towards the*] *Primeval Lightning Field* from O Books.

GJ: What since then?

WA: *Above the Human Nerve Domain*, I think. That's from Pavement Saw Press.

GJ: I just want to make sure I've got your bibliography updated.

WA: I can name a few books if you like. *Impulse & Nothingness* at Green Integer. There is *Alien Weaving*, it's a novella at Green Integer, it's due out. There is *Sri Lankan Loxodrome* that's been due out for some time.

GJ: Sri Lankan what? How do you spell that?

WA: LOXODROME.

GJ: Is that a neologism?

WA: Actually, it's not. I found it, it was a made up term on my part, but I actually found it as a word later on. It was in an older geographical dictionary from 1957.

GJ: Wow. What is it?

WA: As far as I know it had something to do with oblique sailing. It's a nautical term.

GJ: Maybe you have some of your mother's clairvoyance in you? You made up a word and it turns out to be real.

WA: It did look like that. I found out some other things that work like that in the epic poem, "The Henbane Bird." A lot of that came up out of certain towns I came up with in Peru and in Chile. The bird itself, the Henbane bird is really a hummingbird. It is based on an Andean Hill Star. The Andean Hill Star is the second largest hummingbird on earth. It is about seven inches or longer. I've seen one on film. They are quite impressive. The Henbane bird, the Andean hill star, its region of largess is the Andean region. The poem is an interweaving, where you take all these different geographical locales and cosmic locales and the heavens of these locales and all the flora and fauna of the earth. I have located it back to the bird's voice enunciating its own complexity. The reality of the earth and the cosmos combined with environmental threat ... as well as the long-term condition of the human species.

GJ: Do you do that often in your work? I don't know if you would call it a persona or maybe even channeling where you're imagining another voice and writing from that position?

WA: The poem is not a strict monological "I." It is always seek[ing] for other forms and other realities that resound in its energy. I would call it, for want of a better term, planetary scope.

GJ: So it gets you outside yourself?

WA: Absolutely. Because it is not my voice in terms of what I am saying about me but about those other realities flowing through me.

GJ: Why do that? Why do you want to get outside of yourself?

WA: Because it is a way of allowing creativity to circulate, which is not a preplanned creativity, but a creativity that comes through the way water finds its channel. And of course, I am prone to this. You have to be prone to a certain kind of speaking as a poet. You can't be someone else speaking, but I always call it "psychic fecundation." Because everybody carries some kind of fecundation. Just like planets carry fecundation. People carry fecundation.

GJ: Isn't that akin to an aura?

WA: Yes, but also there's always the way one speaks, the way one walks, the temperature one carries, being closer to fire, closer to ice, closer to coolness or darkness, closer to light. It is just like looking at colors. We have all these different phases of color, putting things together. If you just look at the spectrum of colors in a catalog list. As a colorist, as a poet, the words just jump out at you. And you begin to understand that there are all these different shadings and combinations which are really infinite.

GJ: By changing the atmosphere, you can alter what you might be more in tune with?

WA: Once you are in that malleable state, you are able to create endlessly in that regard. All is open to endlessness, in terms of this whole idea of 26 letters of the alphabet becoming infinitely malleable. It's kind of the way the Mayans used a certain set of numbers to work out infinity. You can do that in terms of the letters of the alphabet.

G J: Like the six colors being primary and three secondary colors of the palette?

W A: The same difference.

G J: I want to get back to your sort of metaphysics later, but lets go back to, I want to make sure I have a list of what you've got in press right now. So we ended with *Sri Lankan Loxodrome*. And where is that?

W A: Unplaced at present.

G J: And that's poetry?

W A: Yes

G J: Anything else that is coming up?

W A: *Exobiology as Goddess*, a book of poetry. I think I have it here.

G J: That is one of your favorite words, I've noticed, "exobiology." It's got a great sound, too. And where is *Exobiology as Goddess*?

W A: It is due out from Manifest Press.

G J: You mentioned several years back in that interview with Harryette, a book of drawings. Has that ever come out?

W A: No that hasn't come out yet. But I do have that in mind for the future.

G J: Do you work mostly in pastels on paper?

W A: I always do that. They become paintings in pastels. I am self-taught as an artist. I've never taken a drawing or painting class, ever. So, I've clearly . . .

G J: You've got talent! I mean . . . Do you like to go see art in museums? Do you look at art in books?

W A: Yes, I've always done that. I'm osmotically active in museums, loving painting, absolutely loving it. I am looking forward to getting a space where I can plumb the depths for about six months or ten months as a visual artist. I've never had that luxury before. Everything has been so intense in the last year. But it is definitely something I think about and look forward to. The book of drawings will appear later.

G J: Is there traffic between your art and your poetry? You talk about vision in your writing, but your writing doesn't strike me as visual in the sense in the way you lay it out on the page. Do you see your work as an artist, a visual artist shaping your writing?

W A: No, not in the sense that it's direct, conscious influence, but it would have to have some kind of subconscious relay or subconscious recur2 rence, on both levels. You do both of them. On one level I let them take over and conduct the orchestration between themselves.

G J: Is it a different feeling? You talk about being in a zone when you are writing. Is it the same feeling when you are drawing? Or is it different?

W A: It's the same feeling, but it's like psychologically using your left hand. I'm right-dominant, but I do use my left hand, so I am looking at drawing psychologically as another freedom, or as another escape.

G J: Is your right brain involved?

W A: I am a right brained person. Very right-brain dominant.

G J: You are right handed?

W A: I am right handed. I am right brain dominant. But I do many things with my left hand. So, you know, it is "creative ambidextrousness." I learned that from looking at certain artists, musicians in particular, and artists and painters who wrote. Miró's letters impressed me as well as Dali's early writings. They are very interesting.

G J: Do you like their work as painters?

WA: Oh, I love it. Love it.

GJ: Other favorite artists?

WA: I guess Maurice Vlaminck . . . Bonnard's colors, Soutine, Van Gogh, Matta, Lam, Gorky . . .

GJ: You think mostly of color?

WA: When I do things they are drawn first by pencil. They are drawn first. I actually do the drawing.

GJ: You said, you told Harryette Mullen that when you are drawing a line in pencil you are seeing colors.

WA: I do see colors. And the different lines suggest the colors to me. Absolutely they do. So I can actually see that.

GJ: Does that happen when you are writing? Do you sort of see an image or subject matter? It seems like you do start with the subject matter. And then go from there. When you decide on subject matter, do you see those images or what direction you are going to go? Like you see color on paper?

WA: No, I think for me, it is the ear which is dominant. Like Breton or Blake, you have to have the ear to hear, and the shapes themselves appear.

GJ: Do you read out loud as you are composing?

WA: Never. It is always inside. It is always the inner which is speaking.

GJ: We have been talking sort of about the recent works. Your first book *Vertical Rainbow Climber* came out in the late 80s. So give us the larger picture of your career. How your identity as a poet changed or your selfdefinition in the past 20 or so years?

WA: Not much. I think the seed was always set prior to the time that I wrote. And it has been evolving from day to day, moment to moment, week to week, year to year. I see myself as part of the magical tradition. Magically transmuted or transformative language. You can go back into the early work for that. When in terms of the so-called point, space, time that art ignited—the surrealists got me—I could identify with them only because the way my own internal weather was construed.

WA: I'm always thinking of the traditional culture or the aboriginal cultures that have the same understanding of eternity that I feel. I think in the United States or the West, the prevailing recognition is of somebody always changing, doing this or doing that, but the pulse that keeps them active is that which is unchanging. So if you separate the whole idea of change from the aboriginal content that created it, I think, [it is] a delusion.

GJ: This sort of brings us back to the metaphysic and the mystical in your work. Is this what you mean when you talk about a vertical poetics and the three, as you described it, the three levels of the mind: the subconscious, the superconscious, that sort of verticality. And is the superconscious that which is eternal or unchanging?

WA: I think that all of those are unchanging and developing at the same time. They are not separate. Once you get into the idea of a total world, and you look into a traditional culture, utensils are all charged with this magic, but at the same time partake of utility. What one dreams, one's conscious conduction of the realms of higher consciousness, it is all there. In other words, all these levels are possible and that they all imply one another simultaneously.

GJ: Is it not a like a Freudian fusion.

WA: Not like a Freudian measurement, a Westernized measurement. The latter is becoming less and less applicable at this time.

GJ: Do you practice any spiritual tradition?

WA: Not really as such. Poetry is the practice and writing is the practice for me. I know some people who meditate. I've meditated and done this and done that. It is through language and art that I'm able to stay continuously focused without any break 24 hours a day. It is not an energy I'm abstracting.

GJ: I know you don't like categorical thinking, that it fragments the world. The critics and your readers are going to eventually try to put you on a map. You've mentioned earlier influences, Césaire, Kaufman, Lamantia. Where do you see yourself in relation to your contemporaries? Maybe a better way to ask that question is who is your favorite contemporary writer?

WA: There are a lot of them. In fact, we had a whole host of them here. I organized a surrealism conference here.

GJ: When was that?

WA: I think 2003.

GJ: How did it go?

WA: Ah, it went great. We had quite an incredible array of poets there. Andrew Joron, Lee Ballentine does the great *Ur-Vox* magazine, it is fantastic. There is John Olson, Roberta Olson, Adam Cornford, just to name a few.

GJ: Are most of these people from LA?

WA: No, they're from Seattle and New York City, Washington DC, San Francisco. It was not a local event. Although we did have people from Los Angeles attend, the whole idea was to bring the larger picture into place. And this is why I'm very comfortable doing things here, and I am doing the marketing job here for Beyond Baroque press. We just sent out three of our latest books and getting them put into markets across the country and into Canada. Just got off the phone with The Poetry Project in New York. They stock our books there.

G J: Books of poetry?

W A: Mostly poetry. I will show you copies of them. But, I have another book on the way.

G J: Which one?

W A: It's *Sunrise in Armageddon*.

G J: And where is that coming out from?

W A: Spuyten Duyvil, a powerful press in New York City.

G J: May I have a look at the manuscript?

W A: Go ahead. That's why I brought it.

G J: So do you have to actually sit down and type your longhand out? Or do you have someone else do it?

W A: I do it myself. It's all the corrections. Typos really. I'll give you the spelling of the press, it's SPUYTEN DUYVIL.

G J: Is that one word or two words?

W A: Two words.

G J: Let's talk a little bit more about this surrealism. Most associate surrealism with ironic distance. There seems to be a certain kind of conviction or sincerity in your work. Do you see a distinction between those two terms?

W A: I understand that surrealism is a great energizer, but it has never been a theoretical or abstract circumference inside of which I was buried. To me, it is an imaginative spark, and so I've never been ideological or working with any kind of practical mode in terms of speaking to that. But it is an energy, and I think I have discovered something that is unique and invincible in the realm of its ubiquitous waters.

Surrealism is an energy that seems to supersede itself continuously. It's supercessional energy so powerful it can no longer be confined within a simple school or within a simple definition.

GJ: It is that kind of language when you talk about power and that transcendence or overcoming or liberation. That's what I mean when I talk about that sincerity or conviction in your work. It seems to be something that separates you from some of your contemporaries, particularly Language poets, who might be more ironic. Your weather changes and your voices change in your poems, but it seems like that conviction repeats, is that the right word? It seems to be constant, continuous.

WA: Yes, it's continuous. I am like that red Australisn aborigine I saw in an older *National Geographic*. I could see this glow burning in his skin, and he was an odd one, because I say red because he was an odd one. He was a pure aboriginal but he looked different to me by . . .

GJ: Skin color?

WA: Yes, skin color, but I just mentioned that because of the symbolic of his visual burning and this constancy in burning and so I wanted to point out that he was different, like a human athanor. I am thinking about that, since one is part of, or on another wavelength, so to speak. I don't mean that in an overdramatic way again. Because for me, it is the only way to be. I understand what Bud Powell was going through when all he could do was play piano. Or when the critic asked Eric Dolphy, what are you going to do now that no jobs are in the offing? And he said, I am not going to do anything other than what I am playing. Now I can totally understand that. After living so long in this orbit as a creative person in a very utilitarian society. Possibly the most utilitarian society on earth.

GJ: Last night I was watching in my hotel room a sci-fi . . . I don't know if they did an original version, but a version of "A Brave New World." Freaking me out how true to life that has become, even though that novel was written 30 or 40 years ago. And we haven't heeded that warning at all.

WA: No, no.

GJ: You say that you are not ideological, but you see your writing doing some of that political work of surrealism disrupting that utilitarian culture?

WA: Oh, absolutely. Because the situation is so dire in that regard. It has been for many, many years. Certainly prior to my circumstances. It is something that has to be understood. Not only in this society, but in others as well. This was one of the takes in my book, *Asia & Haiti*. That was a byproduct of my desire to go into each region's political confines in that book. But you see it. There is absolute oppression today. And we see what goes on and has gone on. So you find these different areas that you see across the earth, but it represents that same kind of spirit. So all you have to do is open up the newspaper, and you see the mess this system has become. And I use "mess" quoting from David Bohm, a physicist, who is talking about creativity. And how the continuing epoch of utilitarianism has spawned what he considers this mess. Nothing is original. Everything is a redraft, an update. Simulation of something prior. So to make those first steps out there to something absolutely different and absolutely new, obviously, you can't get support, you are pretty far out there on the wire.

GJ: What difference, then, does poetry make? If it's out there, or people aren't listening to it?

WA: I think poetry is something that is very powerful because of the fact that the poet himself is poetry. And so, it works in many dimensions. When I talk to people, when I contact them, I am contacting them with this energy that I write with. It's not the same exact energy, but it is that energy, it's just in another context. So people can read it, they can experience it through conversation or body language. It has a great relay effect. Because I am into understanding how spores work, knowing that the life on this planet was started outside the confines of the earth. And we have these spores going across the universe continuously. So we're not in a kind of an isolated symmetric or anything like a closed system, it's an open system.

GJ: Does poetry help keep that opening open?

WA: It does keep the opening open and what's happening is that if you look at the bigger picture, which too many people have forgotten how to do—consumed as they are by pure utility—that I think meaningful work, and not only in the area of poetry, but meaningful work is a legacy from which we continue to exist, and will forever. Take the work of Virgil; you can't spend those coinages that he had to handle in his day to day life. But you know the work has outlasted coinages, has outlived the language of Latin itself, has outlasted the so-called practical political concerns of the era. But what I am saying is that great poetry does leap above the aforementioned. Césaire says in an interview that true life is not politics. And he should know, since he's done both of them.

GJ: A related question would be that of ethos. Do you see yourself as an ethical poet? We talked about poetry being your way of being in the world. Is there also a way of being towards others in your poetry? Some sort of . . . hold some of these threads together. Do you see this as an ethical project?

WA: And you mean ethics in terms of?

GJ: I knew you were going to ask that question.

WA: I can't answer this question in the sense that I can't satisfy someone else's idea of what ethics is about. Because this is going to all get ensnared in a host of complications, because, for instance, when you work with the imaginal as energy, when you are working on the subconscious level, when you are working at levels that are far beyond the survival mode, you have to engage these levels in dialogue with people that don't understand them, who are more utilitarian in scope. What is this doing for me now? How much did you make for that? What kind of money are you going to get for what you do?

GJ: Do you get those kinds of questions a lot?

WA: I've gotten them; it is an ongoing condition because of the fact that there is sometimes less than enough income. I think people too are pointed towards disposable income. And that's become part of the whole situation. But, sometimes you are doing work at levels of refined sensitivity, and you are being judged by activity more akin to consumerism. And it is impossible to explain to that particular person at that particular time. You just don't have enough. Now does that make you a bad person? I think, no. Does that make you a questionable person to them? Probably, yes. At that moment. But life is a river and it has ways of correcting and showing other aspects of what you are doing in different contexts that they may be able to relate to in time.

GJ: I don't know about those utilitarian people, but to many young, aspiring poets you are an inspiration in the sense that you've made that choice to live the life of a poet and for that to be your vocation. But how are you making a living right now?

WA: It's difficult. I am working on projects as we speak. You know, I've always had these conditions where I don't need, I don't have enough, or I get too much. It's been fantastic in all areas, including the money. I'd love to advance a tremendous amount, if I got a tremendous amount of capital, you know I already have my values, so the money wouldn't do anything but facilitate what I already am.

GJ: You think in terms of the poetry?

WA: Well, yes of course. I think in terms of creative activity. We're dealing with a situation where people don't understand. I mean, you have people with money, but they don't have the sensibility where the money should go. Or they put it into a yacht or into a television program. Or put it into a TV millionaire ... what's his name with that program?

GJ: With Donald Trump?

WA: Donald Trump, that type of thing. When you really look at it, of course, it is silly. You know that certain things do last, even in a world as chancy as this. And people do work with vibration on deeper levels. In Canada, or England or the United States, Venezuela, you will find these people. They exist right now as we speak. I always talk to people about this; half of the people and more than that in this world will never make a phone call. With any type of telephone. They have no typewriters. They have no basic technology. Billions. We have 5 billion on this earth now? 6 billion? Let's be conservative and say that a billion people have that technology. So this—our phones, our cars—is maybe not a total picture; it's part of a picture. I think we have to put the parts together like David Bohm was talking about. The problem of the age is fragmentation. He looks to deal with the whole condition, not with the partial condition. We are dealing with the partial condition at the present time, as we speak.

GJ: A lot of contemporary writers and great poets and thinkers would say that this "partial condition" is postmodernism; this is the postmodern condition. We should embrace it, maybe we have ironic distance from it, but everything is culturally constructed. It is always changing and you can't fight that. You see that; you seem to be going on a different tack? Some of those notions of things that are eternal or things that last; that's a very modernist way of thinking. That it is almost quaint . . . You might hear that kind of thing. That critique. How would you respond to that?

WA: That it's quaint? That is a problem that really arose actually when the Moorish civilization fell.

GJ: In Africa?

WA: Because of the fact that the Western heritage was spawned there. The Renaissance would never have taken shape without the Moors. That is left out of most histories. They are dealing with an isolated artifact. Why don't they go back 700 years to Granada? Now if you look at the record you know that Greek philosophy was practically lost. Plato, Aristotle, everything. The Moors translated them into Arabic and got them into the Western lexicon, because the monasteries had kept all the manuscripts and were isolated. There was some learning going on in Europe, but after the Empire fell it was pretty much groups of isolated villages. For 300 years marauders coming in killing the villagers. There was no time for any concentrated learning, but in Granada they had concentrated it. In fact, there's an actual count of bookstores in Cordoba in the 10th century; I may have something here about that. Anyway, the basic idea of the whole Renaissance in Spain was that there was a total renaissance. There were hospitals. They actually had street lights in the 950s. Street lighting at night. Everything was organized, and the Jewish, Christian, and Islamic scholars worked together. Do we find that today? Pretty much no. I'm not saying this was a perfect situation, but if there [is] going to be understanding or embracing our present condition something of this spirit needs to ensue in another tenor. It's like Shelley said, that the poet should lead, not follow. A poet is like a shaman and he can go out there and can work with his own hands, in his own writing, his own utterance, to bring vatic temperatures to bear. This is something that Breton was talking about in regard to the future. Opening up those energies, going into alien provinces of the spirit. He goes out to Nevada, he was in Canada and Haiti, he alights in New York. All of his contemporaries from that age like Wolfgang Paalen, Leonora Carrington, Remedios Varo landed in alien meadows. And the same—it was parallel to Césaire creating vatic contagion in Martinique. Can you imagine the modernists in this context? Aldon Nielsen has written in one of his early books about the letters of the Modernists, the early Modernists, and how they took up the racism of the era in the 1910s through 1940s, which includes Eliot, which includes Pound, which includes e.e.cummings. All these people, Wallace Stevens, were part of the racist order. Why do you think somebody like Melvin Tolson was left out, and somebody like Césaire was taken in? It was a different spirit.

GJ: I just spent 10 days in DC looking at Tolson's papers. He had differences with Eliot, but he certainly, he constantly said, "I'm trying to take the form and the strategies of juxtaposition without the politics. I've got a different end to it."

WA: Well, he'd have to. He was coming from a whole different place. But they would never have accepted him. No way. People say we have to separate Pound's work from his politics. You can do that, but there is a strong element of racism in Modernism that was never addressed until recently. But it is in the letters. Unfortunately, they took the racism up. What Breton did—and I am not saying this ideologically, because it is a fact—was he went against the Moroccan Riff War in the 20s. I didn't see people like Pound or Eliot going after the lynchers in the 30s or 40s, saying anything about this problem. I know it's not popular, but it's true. These people think that is quaint. They should turn around again because this is something that in particular the Indian peoples in the United States have been working on, this whole idea of universe. And the reason by the way that you live is that you have a whole system. If one part of the system doesn't work, you become sick. It has become stagnant, right? What are you going to do? Do you need medicine to correct it? Or some kind of herb or some kind or source of, what is the word for it?

GJ: Salve?

WA: Salve or something like that to bring yourself back into focus again. If you look at the newspaper; it is an indicator of, a barometer of the civilization and where it's going to.

GJ: As one poet to another, as one who hasn't found his direction as you have—how do you avoid the sicknesses of the day? Every time period has blind spots. Certainly the Beat poets, for example, of the 1950s, although they may have been open-minded about race—though that is problematic too—some were very homophobic or very sexist. So the thought seems to be something. There is always a potential blind spot. As a poet, how do you avoid those sicknesses?

WA: Well, you don't. I mean that this is another thing—the beauty of the human race is its imperfections. And you can't be totally everything to everybody because maybe at a certain era, we can say that this is racism and that's homophobic, which is true. But that's a blindspot, it's a blindspot. But, my previous statement was that certain people did see that early on, and it wasn't their blindspot. But the poets I feel in league with had their own blindspots too. This is one of the reasons we had this conference on surrealism. The whole focus was to show how surrealism is not looking at history, but is looking at the future. What are we dealing with now, not what they were dealing with in Paris in 1935.

GJ: Can that futurist moment help us avoid disaster, the sickness? I guess I was asking about that futuristic moment you were talking about. Is that one of the ways the poet can heal? Do you see it as the poet's job to look into the future and to somehow lead humankind towards that rather than staying caught in the quagmire or the same old problems?

WA: We can play around with problems, and they can become interesting to a point, but it looks like at a certain point the problem begins to repeat itself. We always pass that problem by and that exercise becomes immediately dated. As always, a great way of looking at the present is that it's open as a medium to the future.

GJ: Is that why you see surrealism as inspiration, but not your main poetics? That some of its problems are dated?

WA: Some of what people think are some of its interworkings are dated. Whom I can talk to. What I can read. What I can't read. I mention this in the context of Breton's leanings in 1964 concerning this new opening, that perhaps surrealism is going into a zone of neutrality to merge at another point. He took a walk with Octavio Paz, and spoke of surrealism entering a neutral state. And of course, we have seen that we are dealing with some very interesting situations now in the world that he was picking up at that point. Then we are going into the space where surrealism supersedes itself. Breton said he'd be the first one to join it. So, in other words, this condition is not static, but a situation that is continuing with momentum. I think that people want to fixate everything into a pattern, so that it can be more recognizable and user-friendly, so to speak. Where you can pick up a work and say that this is 1939 or that that is 1982 or 2004. There are all these demarcations that work in a superficial sense, of course. You can always demarcate things. But, as you know, life is never demarcated and never can be. Really can't be. For instance, this particular war that is being conducted at present. There was an idea and preplanning how it's going to work. And this is not how reality is coming out. This is what you can't do with a poem. You can't really preplan it. Although there are some people who say that you can. But always there is this point something comes in that you didn't know that you'd say. Or some other impulse that has come in that you didn't know how it would work.

GJ: Do you think poetry as a medium is particularly positioned or more open to that otherness and unexpectedness and the unnamable?

WA: Absolutely. Because it is in that sense that you are open to all these images that come upon you from seeming obscurity. All that is living material. Those little meeting points. Those little points that you can't account for. Those synaptic leaps that haven't been planned upon. That's the surprise. That keeps you working and moving.

GJ: I was just about to ask if you were consciously making those choices intentionally in your writing. But that would sort of . . .

WA: You can't really make those choices consciously. I think you can come up with a subject that comes to you and you can begin to work on it, but you don't know exactly how it's going to turn out at every turn, at every nook, at every cranny.

GJ: I guess really the question I really want to ask is to what extent are you open and tolerant of those kinds of gaps, ambiguities, silences, synaptic gaps?

WA: I don't encourage it. They just seem to happen that way, and I do mean that sincerely. I don't really consciously encourage any kind of break up or ecstatic moment or anything like that. I tend to work out of what I have, and there [is] a certain kind of unfolding that takes place with absolute immediacy. But Lorca talked about that second or third hearing. He uses an example of drinking cold water and scribbling black marks in pencil. I mean, waiting for that really true voice. You don't want to get caught up in what your own successful wordplay was at a previous time, and you want to be able to work beyond that. The more you do, obviously the more you find you have to become at one with your own hearing. So you have to hear that deepest trace. I feel I'm working at that deeper trace level at the present time. I hear one level and then I hear it at another level and another level. In other words, when I am doing that I am hearing that deeper trace level, so when I usually work with a text for instance, I'll write it down in longhand. When I go back to type it out, I'll hear it maybe in a different way. A deeper way and that's what I put down. Normally I just do one handwriting and one typewritten, and that's it.

GJ: Do you make a lot of changes in between those?

WA: No.

GJ: You don't find that you need to?

WA: No, I don't. I tend to write it and then let it sit. I let the text set. Some of these texts have sat for years. You have to, like good wood or good wine, let them soak. That is one of the things that doesn't have high value in this kind of society. Because it's how quick you can get things done. How quick can you read? How quick can you dial a phone? How quick can you do anything? Save time. Save time for what? But I don't want to get into that at the present time. I let them soak and I go back and type it out, and I can hear it in a deeper way.

G J: Are you satisfied with the recognition and the exposure you've gotten as a poet?

W A: It's been organic. I can't say anything other than it's been very, very good. I believe in working hard and understanding my limitations and my priorities. But it's been very good in terms of contact from the community. It's great. People like Nate Mackey, Douglas Messerli, Leslie Scalapino—the list goes on and on. You can just name and name and name great people. And I hope to continue to do more with and for the community in the future. It's just been so difficult to survive as a poet, to create the works, to get it out, and then to be able to try to survive and keep yourself intact enough to create. It's quite a struggle. I'm not alone in that. It works in different degrees for different people. But to pursue this art, under the conditions we're under has been quite striking. And I think that poetry will always be pursued. It did survive the camps, and it survived slave-ships and it is continuing to survive. I do believe that it sets up signals that other people are able to pick up on and to begin to work with. Readers that sustain me don't consciously calculate this sustainment. Poetry does work that way. Somebody can be reading my work at 3 a.m. in Toronto because they can't sleep. This is how I communicate. We didn't know each other. That's communicating. But you do have to spend a bit of time in your life doing this. I think poetry is not an extremely young person's art in the sense that it does take time to gain experiences. You can be an old 19 like Rimbaud. You can, because I have seen children that are very, very interesting. At a religious festival in India, and I've only seen it once in film of course. They stick actual pins in the human flesh, walk with this big heavy body tiara. One of the youngest participants to work with this was I think about 7 years old or 8. One of the participants that had done it for the first time was over 70 or something. Anyway, the point being, when you are ready, you're ready. I tend to think—that was a sidebar—I think that the older you are the better you do with this and it's tough on the younger person. It's tough on me to begin to develop and have to have the patience and energy knowing that you need to read more and experience more. It's very important, and you can't just do it after three months of writing. It may be interesting work, but maybe you just need to let it soak. Don't just rush into print. But at the same time, everybody does develop at a certain pace, so I don't want to put that out there as some kind of paradigm—that you have to be old to write. Nothing like that. But you do need to soak up some kind of experience, and I think literature, writing, or poetry doesn't come all at once. It's like a seepage. You know, it's like a water level slowly rises and then it's there. It spills over. It has a currency and other people can see it. I tell people this one thing: You show someone something over here and it's shown to somebody else over there, and they give a similar comment; you've struck an objective current. They were both influenced by the work. And that's why you let the poetry or drawings or paintings go into the world, you don't have to be there to shepherd them and explain them to others. They have this self-communication. Drawings and paintings communicate. We give them up. We're not there—when I write something I pretty much let it go. Pretty much let it go, because I am interested in the new projects I am doing. I am doing a new book right now and I am more interested in that book than anything else, as it should be.

GJ: Tell me about that new project.

WA: Well, it is just a project that I am doing. I've been in transition, and so what I've been doing is finding a work that is able to be worked on at sporadic intervals. It's . . . I call it hermetic autobiography. "Active under Threat" is the provisional name of it.

GJ: I am very interested to see what that—

WA: I am working on listening and hearing its trace elements. It is more like a poetic philosophical text than an actual biography of places, dates, names. I am working with the impulses of periods in my life, which includes the current period and that which is to become. So in that sense it will be a surreal text and I do feel pressure being under threat at the present time. The type of energy I work with every day and the type of environment I am forced to . . . we are forced to partake in, how do you work with that? Because whatever area I am going to go into, I am going to be buffeted. I have to understand that. And that's the one thing people don't understand, that the human being still has the power, even though we look at the technology and it seems over-whelming. But what created that technology? One of the reasons I want to continue to handwrite, is of course the human contact, but also to prove that my mind, the imagination is greater than anything that can be replicated on a machine. There's a seminal essay Philip Lamantia entitled "Poetic Matters" that goes into Bachelard's idea of the "imaginal" and how it leaps outside the journalism of the newspaper space.

GJ: Imaginal. I've seen that word before in your writing.

WA: It's the imaginal, the radiant plane. Where one leaps out into the radiance. It's like the rays of the sun, projecting out to all these different worlds and hidden possibilities. In other words, you're open to possibilities, not involved in a certain type of plagiarized beautification or excellence. It's like doing this; it's like copying a poem out. And I've done this, copying a poem by a Lorca or Gerard Manley Hopkins. You can copy it, but how you do it is a mystery and it remains a mystery. A certain kind of alchemy has to take shape inside of oneself. That is really very site-specific in that sense. It is a mystery, but when it comes out it does harmonize and brings people from all over the world into its purview of readers. But it is not something you can figure out as some type of formula. It isn't really possible to do that. Because if you don't know what's coming up, how can somebody else from a previous poetic incarnation of your work seek to freeze this mystery which is always freshly evolving. It's like looking at a stellar nursery. We can see that it's really in nature. Astronomers have a real understanding of this. Physicists, mathematicians understand this sometimes better than poets. If they know there are certain kinds of elements that are taking place, it is energy that can't be controlled. But it is part of the spectrum. So to me poetry is part of that nature that we are all part of. To me, it's akin to cicadas.They stay in the ground for about 17 years before emerging. That's amazing.

GJ: It is, and something I heard on NPR, is like how they think in prime numbers. It gets them off the rhythm or the life cycles of some of their predators. Things like that. It's amazing.

WA: All of our human knowledge would have to come out of this existence that we're in, not the opposite way. I think we hear so much of this being built and that being created as if through this medium or this culture—that we put the sun in space. It's just the opposite. Once you understand that turning around from the sun putting us here rather than we putting the sun there, then you can begin to operate a certain way and your technology will work better for you than it does now. Right now, it's an obstruction. Everything is a social obstruction, technological obstruction, psychological obstruction, everywhere you can think of. And it's overwhelming at this point. Maybe it's because the media is more cognizant of technology having been splayed across the world. But, at the same time we have this overwhelming capacity that has been developed but without the understanding of how to use the capacity.

G J : There is a certain hubris. A lack of humility.

W A : Absolute hubris at a time when we can ill afford the hubris.

G J : Right. The planet is on the verge of collapsing ecologically.

W A : Of course, and you have to understand too that somebody can say nothing is happening to the climate, but he or she is using a purview of maybe five years, fifty years. For instance, it takes hundreds of millions of years to build up these oil reserves. It's not like something you can turn a light switch on. The climate is irretrievable.

G J : There is this attitude that the Alaska National Wildlife Reserve was put there for us to drill in.

W A : This remains a perspective. But power does shift and things do change. And things are changing rapidly right now as this whole economy has been called into question. There was an interview I saw a few months ago, a professor I think from Cal Tech. His theory was that oil reserves were running really low, and they asked him if we were prepared. And he said absolutely not. So, as things run low, and then you factor in a billion Indians and a billion Chinese people and make them participate in this kind of system, it's going to be a problem. This is not a way of life that can be sustained everywhere. So, we have to understand, it's like people who are fairly educated and somebody's cousin or nephew is dropping out of high school. Those people think that everybody should go to school and get a good position. Some people aren't going to do that. So we have these old ideas that everybody is supposed to do the same thing. I think this is where poetry should be involved, in differences. In understanding differences. I mean understanding that there are certain individualities that need to be left alone. That's what Césaire's point was when he wrote the open letter to Maurice Thorez to leave the Communist Party in 1956. He says that the Caribbean people have a specific tenor that must not be disrupted with this homogenetic idea of the Marxist realm. We have a right to express ourselves as we are. And he could see that the leftist bureaucracies were overwhelming. Césaire's argument with the former surrealist, Louis Aragon, in the early 1950s who says that poetry should be understood by the masses. He wants to eliminate the imagination. He wants to eliminate the splendor of what can be. Once you go on to that preplanning stage, you destroy the creativity. You set up the mechanism for results. Juan Goytisolo said the same thing at another angle. He left the communists in the late 1950s, and said that he had to get out of these comfortable intellectual circles, so he could begin to grow. It is a painful story. His memoirs, *Forbidden Territory* and *Realms of Strife*, have recently been reissued in a single volume. He talks about the process of getting out of his own habit formation. It is very difficult to do. He's done it, and it takes a lot of self-stamina and doubt and courage. This zone of doubt doesn't mean that you are weak, or if you're weak it doesn't mean that you are actually defeated. It is an experience of something that one needs to feel. Once you can go into the feeling of that, without trying to totally resist it, you realize it two or three days later when you wake up stronger. Or you've grown. We're told that we can't be weak in the day to day world, or that we can't lose a particular battle. If you're not looking to grow, you are not looking to experience. That is very much the case, so for me it's been like the experience of what I am through the limitation that I carry. I test limitations daily, which creates a continuous sort of command. But it is not focusing on the successes, they've already been taken care of.

GJ: What are some of your limitations?

WA: For me particularly it's been the things like economics. I've been doing some work in terms of addressing that, but that's been very difficult. I think that is my major problem right now. It has been that. Another thing has been not enough sustained time with other languages because of the fact of the way I developed and the way I write and the way I think, I've been able to get into a certain kind of hearing of my work that continues to pour in all the time. It doesn't leave much room for anything else. In other words I read, and then I write and then I read, and I write and I draw. It's like a continuous cycle. Maybe it's not so bad.

SUNRISE IN ARMAGEDDON

Conducted by Spuyten Duyvil Books

SPUYTEN DUYVIL: How did a novel like *Sunrise in Armageddon* come to be?

WILL ALEXANDER: As with all combinations an initial spark transpires. That spark began its subconscious sustainment from the point of my contact with Sarduy's *Cobra*. Sarduy had created a world where poetry and narrative fused as the horizon line. A narrative which possessed an uncanny sonar, which for me brought all of the hypnotics of the senses into play. I saw it as another tenor of the antinarrative which Beckett had advanced.

SD: So, is this antinarrative something that is vital to you, that advances your exploration of language?

WA: When I first experienced *The Unnamable*, when *Cobra* appeared, I knew such an exploration was possible for me. Simultaneously I came to the realization that the first person focus would be my book long sustainment.

SD: These books were corroborations for you?

WA: They were corroborations in the sense that I knew that if my splintered perch could hold, I could soar, all my disparate angles could fuse by means of the unforeseen.

S D : Disparate angles . . .

W A : Yes—psychology, cinema, the visual arts, poetry, philosophy, music.

S D : You've written in other genres: poetry, plays, philosophy, tales, aphorisms—where would the novel figure in terms of difficulty, in terms of complexification?

W A : As I've advanced in my research, I've found the novel to be the most open, the most flexible form. It has allowed me to place all my forms of writing in one space.

S D : So what in your view kindles or ignites such fusion?

W A : Conviction. The absolute necessity for something to be said as a living inevitability.

S D : Sunrise in Armageddon seems part of a family which we've already touched on. What other books would you include in that lineage?

W A : Goytisolo's *Count Julian*, Bernhard's *Correction*, *Nadja* by Breton, *The Death of Virgil* by Herman Broch. There are others, books which no longer fatigue by means of realism and its attendant paradigms.

INALIENABLE RECOGNITIONS

A lecture given at Beta-Level,

Los Angeles, June 2007

Colonized by the rhetoric of visibility, one turns around in a microbe warren, fighting for status according to forms which accrue from the fleeting frontal body. According to this frontal body one is arrayed in static remnants, in corpse-like postures which devolve into the active snare of concussive social tissue. A social concussive which suppresses and re-suppresses poetic conduction. Within this blinding decurrence one is always summoned by mislaid agendas, by quicksanded mazes, by formal suffocations, all in the service of diabolical cogitos.

As if the sun were missing and retroactively replaced by a blazeless secondary moon, having no other purpose than to give of itself as a scrupulous or functioning disorder. And I am not speaking here of the moon as organic respiration, as a fractal of itself conspiring with suns, but as an isolate technical seduction attempting to burn inside itself, casting in its wake a riddle of broken novae and spectrums.

But if we look at the formation of stars, and mollusks, and cells, we see the interminable hypnotic, the spiral of burning glances, always suggesting by rotation kinetic perpetuity. The understanding here is that the frontal personality is always reaffirmed by the material paradigm as a separable mechanics. And this separable mechanics can be discerned in Descartes or Julius Caesar always operant at a plane where energy erupts as obvious misnomer. Where the clause reacts subduction by subduction according to its substance which generates as a result, a requisite quantity or weight. According to the West quantity or weight is repeatable as history, as a mechanics of didactic armory. A state of being always operable through conflict, through the mesmerism which coils and recoils through thought as a devastating violence.

Within the Western psyche human worth is summoned through conflict, through the clashing of fragments across the ozone. History then accrues as the perfect cholera of density, so that its necessity transpires through heaps of bodies which configure in the rational mind as honed embryos in the breathing. So every detail is counted according to mesmerized biography, according to the minutia which condones the fate of the teeming frontal portion; according to its mass, to its contorted geometrical ascendance, understood as a conquering plan or Kelvin. Space then takes on substance as a conquered proportion, followed by law as racial mimicry, and the result is the prior 7 centuries deduced to the flaws in the Eurocentric confine. Within its laws it defies the recognition of its limits, looking at other pronouncements with ingrained disrecognition.

Conversely, the communal, that which associates the whole with the part, can never carry as its paradigm a priori injury or discomfort. Thus the lemur, and the verdet of the Macaw is simultaneous with the endogenous. Therefore matter cannot be contained as sterilization by plinth, by manipulated allotment or border, this being the core of Asiatic endogeny, and by extension, Africa, with all its stunning oral kingdoms. Thus Africa, within the aforementioned confine remains the food from the coiling leper's tree. So the derma at the darkened leper's tree can never be properly assessed by plinths, by a strictly numeric or technical embodiment. And so the derma darkens and smolders at the root of the Cartesian technical tree. Thus the West can never address such smoldering, never capable of imbibing its laws of the unobservable. It can only address the pylon as a cataract of weighing, as if its gross recognition were the reason for its standing. In other words, observational bounty which no longer lives by originatory breathing or fire. Its is simply an object which concurs with the notions extended through archaeological biographics, a biographics whose parturition is only capable of that which postdates the energies of Moorish Andalusia. I'm speaking of the era of 1498, of 1533. Of course, these are arbitrary dates which burn in the European sensibility as superior conduction. Neural quanta wizens, and the elements are stamped with a monochromatic optical seal.

What Grosseteste thought, what Roger Bacon compounded through that thought became suspect, and was surreptitiously soldiered away by a Dominican order whose efforts conformed to power as piacular achievement. Grosseteste and Bacon, transmitters of dangerous evolvements, were not unlike Moorish cellular arks, transgressing divides, sailing to the port of tremendums. Under the Italian or subsequent Renaissance, Mali and Timbuktu become more and more as the opprobrium absorbed in the color of the thorn bush of the Christos. And we know that the Christos implies a trenchant separation between what is approved and what is disengendered. This in turn becomes a malignant recognition of a penteconter, a galley, with its sails artfully structured with visually threaded cadavers.

Yet how can this galley take in the ice fields, the wildebeest optics, the spontaneous hexagrammatics of the servals? Here I'm simply inscribing a lack which fails at inclusion, not only the summed gargantuan of what I'll call the balletics of the ozone, but at the spillage of the sky vertically exhaling as a burning supra-physical raga. Perhaps one could compare this raga to the fumes from the confounding glimpses of the Pharonic wails of Pakistani ragas. Ragas which spin by means of phosphenic confoundment, like aural spiraling through a macrocosmic ozone. And from its mystery derives fever, a great pyrolatry of charisma.

In this sense one can never engender sterility, or create by its absence a treatise on accrued and culpable voids. As if such voids could be defined and rendered palpable within an exteriorized decalcomania. A decalcomania drawn in the manner of a separable recognition, structured according to seedless invictas.

Let me say this, the person remains his or her own concomitant experiment. In the cellular ground there exists galactic neural depth, as an a priori balance anterior to suns. And it is the nature of the anterior to inculcate the totalic, which includes suns, and planes, and mysteries. For if Descartes were capable of weighing the image in his neural hollows, he would be prone to a privacy where Breton enlivened a verbal proto-hieroglyphics, an ignited sand where savor flares up as bluish irregularity through quanta. The latter remaining a paradigm non-attributable to personality, to a palpability which fuses with the exhaustion of the provinces. Breton signals a zone where the ground no longer merges with ground, where an integral voltage consumes all prior thinking by means of incandescent slippage.

When Miro configures suns which explode, the by-product remains as fount or interior origin. A fire which consumes from inconspicuous arcana, always living in the cells as a molten which transfixes functions.

As someone like Leiris intuitively attests, the nerves invisibly resonate in what the Dogon understands as collective or spiritual genetics. Within such a view each prosthetic of the technical begins taking on the aura of vanishment so as to allow invisibly gathered bodies to aviate through the uranian by means of intuitive cartographics. Because the cells spin, turbulence engenders the open. As if the body had become vapor suffused by the vocables of anterior navigation, so that its kinesis invigors like a pouring of rays from Sirius B.

Saying this, I can do no more than build on the sodium which insists on itself, which understands itself as mean over and beyond the engendered. Over and beyond the chaos inscribed on the horizontal soil, which now calls for an energy over and beyond the zodiac, where a neutron semantics is transpiring.

AFTERWORD

THE NEW ANIMISM

Will Alexander, born in 1948, was raised in Los Angeles and attended UCLA. He alludes to a painful process of self-education in his first book, *Vertical Rainbow Climber*: "Outside myself and bleeding on my own discoveries I discover in a cave Pythagorean lodestones broken in the air of Chaldean snake myths." During those years of self-discovery, Alexander worked mostly in isolation, becoming the conduit for a primal and oracular speech. The visionary writings of Will Alexander participate in, but can hardly be confined to, the pan-African surrealist tradition of Jayne Cortez and Aimé Césaire. The explosion of his language engulfs almost every continent and sweeps away the categories that separate poetry and philosophy, myth and science.

As Garrett Caples has pointed out, "Alexander's surrealism is not about 'the image' but about 'the word.'" Obviously, Alexander's self-fashioning as a poet did not start from that centralizing point of view demanded by scopic discourse. Instead, he positioned himself within the contingent order of the lexicon, refashioning (and thus reclaiming) language word by word. As a result, Alexander's writing liberates the imagination from the restricted economy of the image. The linguistic turn of Alexander's practice melts metaphor and metonymy together to make a new glyph of meaning. This Alexandrian glyph is typically formed by neologisms and etymological dislocations; by "focus throws" between denotation and connotation; and by the radical recontextualization of specialized vocabularies.

At the same time, it is apparent that Alexander does not wish to simply cancel the received meaning of a given word in order to replace it with his own meaning. Alexander's books often include a glossary in which the ori-gin and interrelation of certain words is explained. This practice has evoked the ire of one literary critic who, in a review of Alexander's book-length poem *Asia & Haiti*, complained that "the careful annotation of exoticisms and their seemingly arbitrary deployment within the poem work at cross purposes to one another." While this complaint is misguided, it nonetheless registers the fact that, in Alexander's practice, the meaning of the same word is simultaneously defined and indefinite, setting a vivid dialectic of freedom and determinism in motion within the poem's linguistic order. Once caught up in this dialectic, words no longer can be expected to serve a strictly referential function, or even an allusive one. Along with the significative aspect of words, their purely material aspect as shapes and sounds enters into play in the poem. Words thereby acquire some of the qualities of paint in the works of those surrealist artists who stand on the cusp of abstract expressionism, such as Gorky and Matta. In such artworks, the paint thickens and clots at strategic nodes into a three-dimensional object, then thins and slides away to become a representational medium, playing surface textures against perspectival depth. What the critic perceived as "cross purposes" in Alexander's writing are actually kinetic interactions between referential and nonreferential planes, an important feature of the poet's painterly style. But there is a political corollary to be drawn as well: these interactions tend to resist the encirclement of the imagination by authoritarian forms of discourse. The poet's ability to liberate language in this way is a magic weapon, and part of the spell he is casting against oppression.

We find this stratagem at work also in the present volume. The collection is divided into five sections, the first four treating, in succession, of geopoli-tics, personages, Negritude, and poetics; the last section is comprised of wide-ranging interviews with the author. These diverse articulations are concerned to make an argument that references the world— but only by means of the poetic Word, which exceeds all referential frames.

Throughout the book, Alexander's word operates primarily as an exponent of the world's own self-transforming, self-exceeding power. In his essay "Los Angeles: The Explosive Cimmerian Fish," referencing the uprising provoked by the exoneration of police officers responsible for beating Rodney King, Alexander declares:

> I align myself with the energies inherent in the wild specificity of Brazilian Indians, with the natural ambulations of tarantulas and Caimans, with the nomos of carnivorous Amazonian greenery, with its fire-ants stored in Cecropia trees, with its restless Jaguars and lizards, with its monstrous Acrosoma spiders. Here I am gliding down jagged rapids of sound, clothed with the decorative Peperomia leaves seismically watching the sub-conscious weathers of my brethren, as a former slave society, striking back at degradation, with the anger and force of a partially mutilated piranha.

The diversification of species in the planet's equatorial hot zones is indexed to the question of social justice: "insurrection" is equated with "resurrection." This lightning-like linkage between planetary (indeed, cosmic) scales of being and human social relations is characteristic of Alexander's writing.

In writing and in conversation, one of Alexander's keywords is "leap," designating a leap between ontological levels. Alexander's thinking here appears to be congruent with recent developments in chaos theory and the study of complex systems. Whether living or nonliving, complex systems exist far from equilibrium, poised on the cusp between chaos and order. The swirl of motion within such assemblages is nonlinear: local causes can bring about nonlocal, systemwide effects.[1] Eventually, a system of this kind will undergo a "phase transition" (Alexander's "leap") to a radically different configuration. At the brink of a phase transition, "the system organizes itself toward the critical point where single events have the widest possible range of effects."[2] Such a system is capable of overspilling its own boundary conditions, resulting in an ontological breakthrough.

This, I believe, is the structure of poetic inspiration as well as of social revolution. The Word is made new in the same way that the World is made new: in response to a flux of energy, the agitation of the Parts increases to the point where the structure of the Whole is overthrown. Abruptly, the world-system, the word-system, arrives at a phase transition, moving as if from a frozen to a fluid state. A poem, by saying the unsayable, brings about a nonlinear circulation of meaning that exceeds the boundary conditions of conventionalized discourse; likewise, an insurrection may be defined as a swift and spontaneous self-organization of the multitude, who take action in ways that exceed the boundary conditions of the social order.

The moment of the phase transition is marked by the onset of tur-bulence, when causality turns fractal, i.e., self-similar at all scales of the system. At this moment, "single events have the widest possible range of effects." In a poem, the meaning of each word becomes maximally open-ended, exquisitely sensitive to and reciprocally tuned by the meanings of all other words; likewise, at the beginning of an insurrection, there's sud-denly "something in the air" that everybody feels and understands at once. In reference to the uprising in Los Angeles, Alexander writes:

> I then stepped from the store into the street and immedi-ately noticed that the people were galvanic with telepathy. And they understood their resurrection as coming from the passionate concentration of flame. . . . [D]uring the revolt, a Rubicon has been crossed, and we have witnessed the telepathic artistry of revenge, the molecules of rebel-lion, which, because of optimum social deterioration, have exploded into a metamorphosis of nightmares. . . .

Earlier in this essay, Alexander describes "The oppressed, the out-raged, without warning, standing like magical lightning bolts, like boil-ing arithmetical titans, their uncanny stumbling quickly focused and sinister, guided by the forces of exponential resurrection." This is the way the world remakes itself: system-transforming change occurs not by gradual accretion, but by spontaneous leaps. Abruptly, the symme-tries associated with a state of equilibrium break down, releasing a cas-cade of unpredictable and unprecedented events: the Big Bang, biologi-cal speciation, political revolution, poetic revelation.

In the present collection of essays and interviews, Alexander under-takes an inventory of the ever-widening cracks in modernity—and meas-ures, by the volatility of the poetic word, the gathering forces of a Great Transfor-mation. Here, energy is shown to be the physical equivalent of imagination as it struggles perpetually against confinement. Anticipating a collective leap of human consciousness comparable to the Mind's original emergence in Africa, Alexander reports on the "world as it is today" as if from a stand-point in the future, from an alterity in which this momentous leap has already occurred.

As the partisan of energy as a form of imagination, Alexander relentlessly critiques linear conceptions of cause and effect, along with all mechanistic modalities of thought and practice. Mechanistic systems here represent en-slavements of energy, the imposition of gridlike coordinate patterns upon a free-flowing and infinite substance. Alexander upholds Surrealism and African animism, in particular, as exemplary of the imagination engaged in struggle against what Manuel De Landa has called "linear equilibrium structures."[3]

For Alexander, animism—as a form of energy/imagination that overflows the boundaries between self and other, human and nonhuman—continues to animate the cultural expressions of the African diaspora, from the blues in North America to the poetics of Negritude in the Caribbean. In effect, Alexander reverses the polarity of Adorno and Horkheimer's pessimistic *Dialectic of Enlightenment* by arguing that structures of oppression in turn produce counter-movements "awash in elusive complexity" and charged with emancipatory potential. As Alexander states in his essay on "A New Liberty of Expression" (included in this volume):

> The continuous attack upon the Afro-American remains a psycho-emotional constant. . . . yet because of this, our imaginations are always awash in elusive complexity. . . . As Césaire has pointed out, Surrealism sparked the African in him. And I can say much the same, in that it has liberated my animistic instinct, so that I am able with unlim-

ited range to roam throughout my writing. Be it radiolarians, or ocelots, or dictators who have merged with dissolution, the whole of life burns for me, existing without border or confinement.

Again, Alexander's re-animistic thought and practice can be related to the scientific paradigm shift initiated by chaos and complexity theory, in which phenomena such as self-organization and other complexly adap-tive behavior—previously attributed only to consciousness and life—have been observed to occur in nonconscious, nonliving systems as well. The border between life and nonlife is now understood to be porous: nonlinear flows of matter and energy are liable to exhibit "emer-gent," or ontologically innovative, self-modifying and self-reproducing behavior at every level of cosmic being. Whenever the equilibrium of a given system is disturbed, matter/energy becomes, in Deleuzean terms, deterritorialized, and roams nomadically throughout the "phase space" (the space of possibilities) of that system. The universe comes alive in disequilibrium.

Here, then, singing in magnetic hoofbeat, are ample evidences of the new, nomadic animism.

ANDREW JORON / BERKELEY, 2008

NOTES

LOS ANGELES: THE EXPLOSIVE CIMMERIAN FISH

1. Guénon, René. "The Language of Birds." *Studies in Comparative Religion,* Vol. 3 No. 2. (Spring, 1969).

A GALLERY COEXISTENT WITH INSPIRATION

This text was first published in *Callaloo* 22 no. 2 (Spring 1999).

All quotations are from Joyce Thigpen, owner of Gallery Tanner. The author notes that the gallery is no longer in operation, and that he was put into contact with the gallery by Angeline Butler.

A SMALL BALLETIC HIVE

This text was first published in *Witz* 7.1 (Spring 1999).

1. De Bono, Edward. *Lateral Thinking: Creativity Step-by-Step.* (Harper Paperbacks, 1973). [Other citations throughout the text are from the same source].

IGNITING THE INWARD PRODIGY

This text was first publshed in *Third Mind: Creative Writing Through Visual Art.* Edited with an introduction by Kristin Prevallet and Tonya Foster. New York: Teachers & Writers Collaborative, 2002.

AGAINST THE STATE AND ITS FUTURE AS A HOMICIDAL ENCLAVE

[Sources for the quoted material on Guatemala in this text could not be located].

1. Bakunin, Mikhail. *Federalism, Socialism, Anti-Theologism.* 1867.

2. Smulkis, Michael and Fred Rubenfeld. *Starlight Elixirs & Cosmic Vibrational Healing.* C.W. Daniel Co, 1992.

CURRENT EMPIRE AS NEMESIS

[Exact citations are unavilable. The author recalls that the bulk of this material is cited from a mid-90s issue of *Foreign Affairs*].

CHINA: MODERN ASPIRATION AS MORASS

This text was first published in *River City* (Spring 1996). Citations in this essay are a collage of phrases from the following sources:

Gore, Rick. "Journey to China's Far West." *National Geographic.* March 1980.

How-Mon, Wong. "Peoples of China's Far Provinces." *National Geographic.* March 1984.

Putnam, John J. "China's Opening Door." *National Geographic.* July 1983.

Topping, Audrey R. "Three Gorges Gamble." *Foreign Affairs.* September/October, 1995.

Waldron, Arthur. "After Deng the Deluge." *Foreign Affairs.* September/October, 1995.

THE EMBLAZONED ONTOGENIC

This text was first published in *Ribot* no. 3. Citations in the text are from:

Diop, Cheikh Anta. "Africa: Cradle of Humanity," in Ivan Van Sertima (ed.), *Nile Valley Civilizations.* Morehouse College, 1984.

CONCRETE: A UBIQUITOUS BUT VEXATIOUS PRAGMATIC

[With the following exception, citations were unavailable for quoted material in this text].

1. Hubert, Renée. *Magnifying Mirrors: Women, Surrealism, and Partnership.* University of Nebraska Press, 1994.

AT THE DEPTH OF THE RADIOLARIANS

Citations in this text are from:

Ray, Carleton and Elgin Ciampi. *The Underwater Guide to Marine Life.* Barnes, 1956.

CHARLES FOURIER: SPARK OF THE HARMONIAN LIGHTNING WHEEL

Citations in this text are from the following sources:

Breton, Andre. *Ode to Charles Fourier.* trans. by Kenneth White. Jonathan Cape, 1969.

White, Kenneth. Translator's introduction to *Ode to Charles Fourier.*

This essay was originally published in *Sulfur* 33, edited by Eliot Weinberg.

ACKNOWLEDGMENT

This text was first published in *Apex of the M* no. 6 (1997).

It now stands as a memorial to the author's father, Will Alexander (1912–1998).

NATHANIEL MACKEY: "AN ASHEN FINESSE"

This text was first published in *Callaloo* 23 no. 2 (Spring 2000).

FOR LAURENCE WEISBERG

This text was first published online in *Milk Magazine* vol. 7 (2003). www.milk-mag.org. Citations are from the poetry of Laurence Weisberg.

RE-EMERGENCE FROM THE CATACOMBS

This text first appeared as the introduction to K. Curtis Lyle, *Electric Church.* Beyond Baroque Books, 2003. Citations are from Lyle's text.

BEAH RICHARDS

Citations in this text are from Beah Richards' obituary.

JOHNNY SEKKA: PARAGON OF THE IMMACULATE

Citations in this text are from Sekka's obituary.

THE FOOTNOTES EXPLODED

This text was first published in *Conjunctions* 29 (2001).

1. Cited in Henderson, David. Editor's note to *Cranial Guitar: Selected Poems by Bob Kaufman.* Coffee House Press, 1996. 2. Kaufman, Bob. "I, Too, Know What I Am Not." *Solitudes Crowded with Loneliness.* New Directions, 1965.

3. *Ibid.* "Camus: I Want to Know."

4. *Ibid.* "Sullen Bakeries of Total Recall."

5. *Ibid.* "To My Son Parker, Asleep in the Next Room."

6. *Ibid.*

7. *Ibid.*

8. *Ibid.* "Camus: I Want to Know."

9. *Ibid.* "Jail Poems."

10. *Ibid.* "Second April."

11. *Ibid.* "Plea."

12. Kaufman, Bob. "Sheila." *Golden Sardine.* City Lights, 1967.

13. *Ibid.* "Lost Window."

14. Rimbaud, Arthur. "Bad Blood." *A Season in Hell & The Drunken Boat.* trans. by Louise Varese. New Directions, 1961.

15. Damon, Maria. "'Unmeaning Jargon'/Uncanonized Beatitude: Bob Kaufman, Poet." *South Atlantic Quarterly* 87:4 (1988).

PHILIP LAMANTIA: PERPETUAL INCANDESCENCE

This text was first published in *The Poetry Project Newsletter* (October/November, 2005).

ABOVE A MARRED POETIC ZODIAC AND ITS CONFINES

With the following exceptions, quotations throughout this text are from Nielsen, Aldon. *Reading Race: White American Poets and the Racial Discourse in the Twentieth Century.* University of Georgia Press, 1990.

1. Garcia Lorca, Federico. "The King of Harlem." *The Selected Poems of Federico Garcia Lorca.* trans. by Donald Allen and W. S. Merwin. New Directions, 2005. 2. Césaire, Aimé. "Return to My Native Land." *Collected Poems of Aimé Césaire.* trans. by Clayton Eshleman and Annette Smith. University of California Press, 1983.

3. Bachelard, Gaston. *On Poetic Imagination and Reverie.* trans. by Colette Gaudin. Bobbs-Merrill, 1971.

THE CARIBBEAN: LANGUAGE
AS TRANSLUCENT IMMINENCE

This text was first published in *Mr. Knife, Miss Fork* no. 1. Sun & Moon, 1998.

1. Erickson, John D. "Maximin's L'Isolé Soleil and Caliban's Curse." *Callaloo* Vol. 15, No. 1. (Winter, 1992).

2. Cited by Erickson.

3. Jackson, John G. *Ages of Gold and Silver.* American Atheist Press, 1990.

SINGING IN MAGNETIC HOOFBEAT

1. Garon, Paul. *Blues and the Poetic Spirit.* City Lights, 1996.

2. Freud, cited by Garon.

A NEW LIBERTY OF EXPRESSION

This text was first published in *Tripwire* no. 5 (Fall 2001).

1. Hilliard, Asa G. "Kemetic Concepts in Education." *Nile Valley Civili-zations: Proceedings of the Nile Valley Conference, Atlanta, Sept. 26-30.* Edit-ed by Ivan Van Sertima. New Brunswick: Journal of African Civilizations, 1984.

ALCHEMY AS POETIC KINDLING

1. Césaire, Aimé. *Collected Poems of Aimé Césaire.* trans. by Clayton Eshleman and Annette Smith. University of California Press, 1983.

2. Rukeyser, Murial. Introduction to Octavio Paz, *Configurations.*

3. Kaufman, Bob. *Solitudes Crowded with Loneliness.* City Lights, 1965.

4. Cirlot, J.E. *A Dictionary of Symbols.* Dover Publications, 2002.

5. Kaufman, ibid.

6. Cited by Octavio Paz, introduction to *Mexican Poetry.* ed. by Samuel Beckett. Grove Press, 1995.

EXACTITUDE

This text was first published in *Beyond Baroque* vol. 28 no. 2.

POETRY: ALCHEMICAL ANGUISH AND FIRE

This text was first published in *O•blek: Writing from the New Coast* (1993).

TRANSGRESSION OF GENRE AS VITALITY

1. Knight, Paul. Introduction to Lautréamont, *Maldoror and Other Poems.* 1998.

VENTRILOQUAL LABOR

This text was first published in *Ur-Vox* no. 1 (2001).

1. Arguelles, Jose. *The Mayan Factor: Path Beyond Technology.* Bear & Company, 1987.

THE ZONE ABOVE HUNGER

This text was first published in *Lipstick Eleven* no. 2 (2001).

HAULING UP GOLD FROM THE ABYSS

This text was first published in *Callaloo* vol. 22, no. 2 (Spring 1999).

1. Author's note: Majied Mahadi, who has since passed on.

WILL ALEXANDER: A PROFOUND INVESTIGATION

This text was first publshed in *The Poetry Project Newsletter* (February/ March, 2005). Notes were assembled by Durand and Alexander.

1. Sage, prophet, and wandering monk Swami Vivekananda (18631902).

2. "... the moon of each of the bodies' vibrations is understood as the flower of spontaneous carbon embodied in the impelling elusives of pure experience itself." "Isolation and Gold," *Towards the Primeval Lightning Field,* O Books, 1998.

3. The largest mountain in the solar system, over three times the size of Mount Everest.

4. "Hauling Up Gold from the Abyss: An Interview with Will Alexan-der," *Callaloo*, Spring 1999. [Included in this volume].

5. Author of *Math: A Rich Heritage* and *African and African-American Contributions to Mathematics*.

6. Senegalese scientist and historian, author of many books, including *The African Origin of Civilization: Myth or Reality*.

7. An ancient name for Egypt.

8. An early (1214–1294) English philosopher, also known as Doctor Mirabilis, considered one of the first advocates of modern scientific methods.

9. Early (1175–1253) English statesman, theologian, mathematician and physicist.

10. The Griffith Observatory in Los Angeles, CA.

11. "Isolation and Gold."

12. Ananda K. Coomaraswarry, "Beauty of Mathematics: A Review," *Art Bulletin*, Volume XXIII, New York, 1941.

13. A number, represented by the Greek letter "Phi" and also known as the "divine proportion" or the "magic ratio," in which the smaller dimension is to the greater as the greater to the whole. It is found throughout the natural world.

ALCHEMICAL DADA: AN INTERVIEW WITH WILL ALEXANDER

Selections from this interview first appeared in *Rain Taxi* (Summer 2006 print edition).

INALIENABLE RECOGNITIONS

This text was first published in *The Jivin' Ladybug* №2: jivinladybug.word press.com/2011/04/23/will-alexander-inalienable-recognitions (2007).

AFTERWORD: THE NEW ANIMISM

1. "Many composite [i.e., complex] systems naturally evolve to a criti-cal state in which a minor event starts a chain reaction that can affect any number of elements in the system. . . . Furthermore, composite systems never reach equilibrium but instead evolve from one meta-stable state to the next." Per Bak and Kan Chen, "Self-Organized Criticality," *Scientific American* (January 1991), p. 26.

2. Paul Cilliers, *Complexity and Postmodernism* (London: Routledge, 1998), p. 96.

3. "Even though the world is inherently nonlinear and far from equilib-rium, its [socioeconomic] homogenization meant that those areas that had been made uniform began behaving objectively as linear equilibrium struc-tures, with predictable and controllable properties. In other words, West-ern societies transformed the objective world (or some areas of it) into the type of structure that would 'correspond' to their theories" (Manuel De Landa, *A Thousand Years of Nonlinear History* [New York: Zone Books, 1997], p. 278). I have argued that such attempts to freeze the structure of the world through the imposition of globalized systems of power inevitably will be defeated by reality's inherent nonlinearity. See the essay "Terror Conduction" in my col-lection *The Cry at Zero: Selected Prose* (Denver: Counterpath, 2007).